ARMOUR & WEAPONS

[*Photograph by Hauser & Menet.*

Armour of Philip II. Madrid.

ARMOUR & WEAPONS

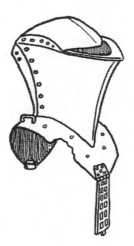

CHARLES FFOULKES

WESTHOLME
Yardley

Originally published in 1909 by Oxford at the Clarendon Press
First Westholme Paperback
© 2005 Westholme Publishing

Published by
Westholme Publishing, LLC
Eight Harvey Avenue
Yardley, Pennsylvania 19067
www.westholmepublishing.com

ISBN: 1-59416-022-8

First Printing
0 9 8 7 6 5 4 3 2 1

Printed in the United States of America
on acid-free paper

PREFACE

WRITERS on Arms and Armour have approached the subject from many points of view, but, as all students know, their works are generally so large in size, or, what is more essential, in price, that for many who do not have access to large libraries it is impossible to learn much that is required. Then again, the papers of the Proceedings of the various Antiquarian and Archaeological Societies are in all cases very scattered and, in some cases, unattainable, owing to their being out of print. Many writers on the subject have confined themselves to documentary evidence, while others have only written about such examples as have been spared by time and rust. These latter, it may be noted, are, in almost all cases, such as the brasses and effigies in our churches, quite exceptional, representing as they do the defences and weapons of the richer classes. What the ordinary man wore, how he wore it, and how it was made are all questions worthy of attention. The works of our greatest romancers have so little regarded the development of armour, and even to-day such anachronisms are seen in pictures and books, that though many comfortable and picturesque notions may be disturbed by the actual truth, yet the actual truth will be found to be no less interesting than fiction. A handy work, not excessive in size or price, and giving really correct information, seems therefore to be needed and should be popular. Such a work is this which Mr. ffoulkes has undertaken, and if we recognize what an immense amount of information has to be condensed within the limits of a handbook, I think we shall fully appreciate his endeavours to give an appetite for larger feasts.

DILLON.

TOWER OF LONDON ARMOURIES.

CONTENTS

AUTHOR'S NOTE

AT the request of many of those who attended my course of lectures, delivered before the University of Oxford during the Lent Term, 1909, I have collected and illustrated some of the more important notes dealing with the Development of European Defensive Armour and Weapons. These pages are not a mere reprint of those lectures, nor do they aspire to the dignity of a History of Armour. They are simply intended as a handbook for use in studying history and a short guide to the somewhat intricate technicalities of the Craft of the Armourer.

No work, even of the smallest dimensions, can be produced at the present day without laying its author under a deep sense of indebtedness to Baron de Cosson for his numerous notes on helms and helmets, and to Viscount Dillon for his minute and invaluable researches in every branch of this subject. To this must be added a personal indebtedness to the latter for much assistance, and for the use of many of the illustrations given in this work and also in my course of lectures.

CHARLES FFOULKES.

The following works should be consulted by those who wish to study the subject of Armour and Weapons more minutely :—

A Critical Inquiry into Ancient Armour, Sir Samuel Meyrick ; *A Treatise on Ancient Armour*, F. Grose ; *Ancient Armour*, J. Hewitt ; *Arms and Armour*, Lacombe (trans. by Boutell) ; *Arms and Armour*, Demmin (trans. by Black) ; *Armour in England*, Starkie Gardner ; *Waffenkunde*, Wendelin Boeheim ; *Guida del Amatore di Armi Antiche*, J. Gelli ; *Dictionnaire du Mobilier Français* (vols. ii and vi), Viollet-le-Duc ; *Encyclopedia of Costume*, Planché ; *A Manual of Monumental Brasses*, Haines ; *Engraved Illustrations of Antient Armour*, Meyrick and Skelton ; *Monumental Effigies*, Stothard ; *The Art of War*, C. W. C. Oman ; *Archaeologia, The Archaeological Journal, The Proceedings of the Society of Antiquaries*; the Catalogues of the Armouries of Vienna, Madrid, Paris, Brussels, Turin, Dresden ; the Wallace Collection, London and Windsor Castle.

The author is indebted to the publishers of Wendelin Boeheim's *Waffenkunde* for the use of the illustrations 33 and 35, and to Messrs. Parker, publishers of Haines's *Monumental Brasses*, for the figures on Plate III.

INTRODUCTION

As a subject for careful study and exhaustive investigation perhaps no detail of human existence can be examined with quite the same completeness as can the defensive armour and weapons of past ages. Most departments of Literature, Science, and Art are still living realities ; each is still developing and is subject to evolution as occasion demands ; and for this reason our knowledge of these subjects cannot be final, and our researches can only be brought, so to speak, up to date. The Defensive Armour of Europe, however, has its definite limitations so surely set that we can surround our investigations with permanent boundaries, which, as far as human mind can judge, will never be enlarged. We can look at our subject as a whole and can see its whole length and breadth spread out before us. In other aspects of life we can only limit our studies from day to day as invention or discovery push farther their conquering march ; but, in dealing with the armour of our ancestors, we know that although we may still indulge in theories as to ancient forms and usages, we have very definitely before us in the primitive beginnings, the gradual development, the perfection, and the decadence or passing away, an absolutely unique progression and evolution which we can find in no other condition of life.

The survival of the fittest held good of defensive armour until that very fitness was found to be a source rather of weakness than of strength, owing to changed conditions of warfare ; and then the mighty defences of steel, impervious to sword, lance, and arrow, passed away, to remain only as adjuncts of Parade and Pageant, or as examples in museums of a lost art in warfare and military history. As an aid to the study of History our interest in armour may be considered perhaps rather sentimental and romantic than practical or useful. But, if we consider the history of the Art of War, we shall find that our subject will materially assist us, when we remember that the growth of nations and their fortunes, at any rate till recent times, have depended to a large extent on the sword and the strength of the arm that wielded it.

There is another aspect of historical study which is of some importance, especially to those who stand on the outskirts of the subject. This aspect one may call the 'realistic view'. The late Professors York Powell and J. R. Green both insisted on the importance of this side of the subject; and we cannot but feel that to be able to visualize the characters of history and to endow them with personal attributes and personal equipment must give additional interest to the printed page and other documentary evidences. When the study of defensive armour has been carefully followed we shall find that the Black Prince appears to us not merely as a name and a landmark on the long road of time; we shall be able to picture him to ourselves as a living individual dressed in a distinctive fashion and limited in his actions, to some extent, by that very dress and equipment. The cut of a surcoat, the hilt of a sword, the lines of a breastplate, will tell us, with some degree of accuracy, when a man lived and to what nation he belonged; and, at the same time, in the later years, we shall find that the suit of plate not only proclaims the individuality of the wearer, but also bears the signature and individuality of the maker; a combination of interests which few works of handicraft can offer us.

From the eleventh to the end of the fourteenth century we have but a few scattered examples of actual defensive armour and arms; and the authenticity of many of these is open to doubt. The reason for this scarcity is twofold. Firstly, because the material, in spite of its strength, is liable to destruction by rust and corrosion, especially when the armour is of the interlinked chain type which exposes a maximum surface to the atmosphere. A second reason, of equal if not greater importance, is the fact that, owing to the expense of manufacture and material, the various portions of the knightly equipment were remade and altered to suit new fashions and requirements. Perhaps still another reason may be found in the carelessness and lack of antiquarian interest in our ancestors, who, as soon as a particular style had ceased to be in vogue, destroyed or sold as useless lumber objects which to-day would be of incalculable interest and value.

For these reasons, therefore, we are dependent, for the earlier periods of our subject, upon those illuminated manuscripts and sculptured monuments which preserve examples of the accoutrements of the twelfth and thirteenth centuries. Of these, as far as reliability of date is concerned, the incised monumental brasses and sculptured effigies in our churches are the best guides, because they were produced shortly after the death of the persons they represent, and are therefore more likely to be correct in the details of dress and equipment ; and, in addition, they are often portraits of the deceased.

Illuminated manuscripts present more difficulty. The miniature painter of the period was often fantastic in his ideas, and was certainly not an antiquary. Even the giants of the Renaissance, Raphael, Mantegna, Titian, and the rest, saw nothing incongruous in arming St. George in a suit of Milanese plate, or a Roman soldier of the first years of the Christian epoch in a fluted breast-plate of Nuremberg make. Religious and historical legends were in those days present and living realities and, to the unlearned, details of antiquarian interest would have been useless for instructive purposes, whereas the garbing of mythical or historical characters in the dress of the period made their lives and actions seem a part of the everyday life of those who studied them.

This being the case, we must use our judgement in researches among illustrated manuscripts, and must be prepared for ana-chronisms. For example, we find that in the illustrated Froissart in the British Museum, known as the 'Philip de Commines' copy,[1] the barrier or 'tilt' which separated the knights when jousting

[1] Harl. MS. 4379, Brit. Mus.

is represented in the Tournament of St. Inglevert. Now this tournament took place in the year 1389 ; but Monstrelet tells us [1] that the tilt was first used at Arras in 1429, that is, some forty years after. This illustrated edition of Froissart was produced at the end of the fifteenth century, when the tilt was in common use ; so we must, in this and in other like cases, use the illustrations not as examples of the periods which they record, but as delineations of the manners, customs, and dress of the period at which they were produced.

The different methods of arming were much the same all over Europe ; but in England fashions were adopted only after they had been in vogue for some years in France, Italy, and Germany. We may pride ourselves, however, on the fact that our ancestors were not so prone to exaggeration in style or to the over-ornate so-called decoration which was in such favour on the Continent during the latter part of the sixteenth and the first half of the seventeenth centuries.

For a fuller study of this subject Sir Samuel Meyrick's great work on Ancient Armour is useful, if the student bears in mind that the author was but a pioneer, and that many of his statements have since been corrected in the light of recent investigations, and also that the Meyrick collection which he so frequently uses to illustrate his remarks is now dispersed through all the museums of Europe. Of all the authorities the most trustworthy and most minute and careful in both text and illustrations is Hewitt, whose three volumes on Ancient Armour have been the groundwork of all subsequent works in English. Some of the more recent writers are prone to use Hewitt's infinite care and research without acknowledging the fact ; but they have very seldom improved upon his methods or added to his investigations. For the later periods, which Hewitt has not covered so fully as he has the earlier portion of his subject, the *Catalogues Raisonnés* of the various museums of England and Europe will assist the student more than any history that could possibly be compiled.

[1] vi. 333, trans. Johnes, 1810.

CHAPTER I

THE AGE OF MAIL (1066–1277)

WITH the Norman Conquest we may be said, in England, to
enter upon the iron period of defensive armour. The old, semi-
barbaric methods were still in use, but were gradually superseded
by the craft of the smith and the metal-worker. This use of iron
for defensive purposes had been in vogue for some time on the
Continent, for we find the Monk of St. Gall writing bitterly on the
subject in his *Life of Charlemagne.* He says: 'Then could be
seen the Iron Charles, helmed with an iron helm, his iron breast
and his broad shoulders defended by an iron breastplate, an iron
spear raised in his left hand, his right always rested on his uncon-
quered iron falchion. The thighs, which with most men are
uncovered that they may the more easily ride on horseback, were
in his case clad with plates of iron: I need make no special
mention of his greaves, for the greaves of all the army were of
iron. His shield was of iron, his charger iron-coloured and iron-
hearted. The fields and open places were filled with iron, a people
stronger than iron paid universal homage to the strength of iron.
The horror of the dungeon seemed less than the bright gleam
of the iron. "Oh the iron, woe for the iron," was the cry of
the citizens. The strong walls shook at the sight of iron, the
resolution of old and young fell before the iron.'

The difficulty of obtaining and working metal, however, was such
that it was only used by the wealthy, and that sparingly. The more
common fashion of arming was a quilted fabric of either linen or
cloth, a very serviceable protection, which was worn up to the end
of the fifteenth century. Another favourite material for defensive
purposes was leather. We read of the shield of Ajax being composed of seven tough ox-hides, and the word 'cuirass' itself

suggests a leather garment. Now, given either the leather or
the quilted fabric, it is but natural, with the discovery and use
of iron, that it should have been added in one form or another
to reinforce the less rigid material. And it is this reinforcing
by plates of metal, side by side with the use of the interlaced
chain armour, which step by step brings us to the magnificent
creations of the armourer's craft which distinguish the fifteenth
and sixteenth centuries.

Sir Samuel Meyrick[1] leads us into endless intricacies with his
theories of the various kinds of defensive armour in use at the
time of the Conquest ; but these theories must of necessity be
based only upon personal opinion, and can in no way be borne
out by concrete examples. If we take the pictured representations
of armour as our guide we find certain arrangements of lines which
lead us to suppose that they indicate some peculiar arrangement
of metal upon a fabric. The first and oldest of these varieties is
generally called ' Scale ' or Imbricate armour. We find this
represented on the Trajan Column, to give only one of the many
examples of its use in very early times. That it was a very pliant
and serviceable defence we may judge from the fact that, with
some alteration in its application, it formed the distinguishing
feature of the Brigandine of the fifteenth century. The scales were
sewn upon a leather or quilted garment, the upper row overlapping
the lower in such a manner that the attachment is covered and
protected from injury (Plate I, 1). The scales were either formed
with the lower edge rounded, like the scales of a fish, or were
feather-shaped or square.

Another method of reinforcing the leather defence has been
named the ' Trellice ' coat. It is always difficult to discover
exactly what the primitive draughtsman intended to represent
in the way of fabrics, and it is quite open to question whether
these diagonal lines may not merely suggest a quilting of linen or
cloth. If it is intended to represent leather the trellice lines would
probably be formed of thongs applied on to the groundwork with

[1] *Archaeologia*, xix. 128–30.

PLATE I

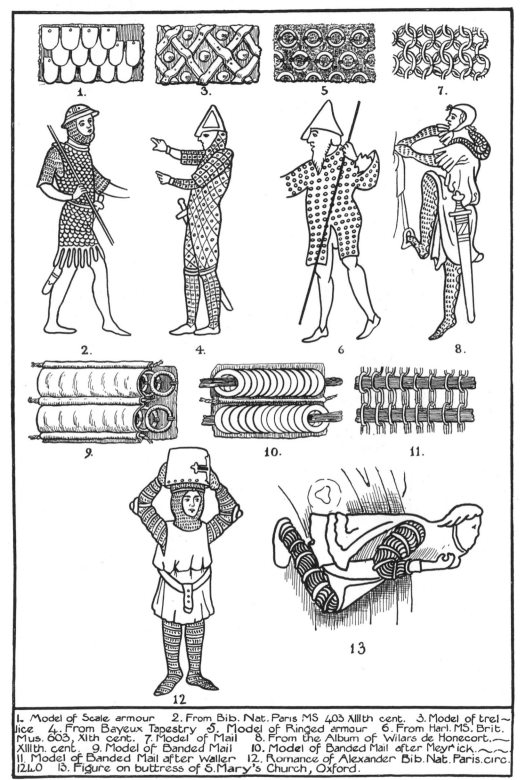

1. Model of Scale armour   2. From Bib. Nat. Paris MS 403 XIIIth cent.   3. Model of trel~lice   4. From Bayeux Tapestry   5. Model of Ringed armour   6. From Harl. MS. Brit. Mus. 603, XIth cent.   7. Model of Mail   8. From the Album of Wilars de Honecort.⏤XIIIth. cent.   9. Model of Banded Mail   10. Model of Banded Mail after Meyrick. ⏤ 11. Model of Banded Mail after Waller   12. Romance of Alexander Bib. Nat. Paris. circ. 1240   13. Figure on buttress of S. Mary's Church, Oxford.

metal studs riveted in the intervening spaces (Plate I). This arrangement of lines is very common on the Bayeux Tapestry.

Another variety to be found in early illuminated manuscripts goes by the name of ' Ringed ' armour. It is quite probable that the circular discs may have been solid, but on the other hand, from the practical point of view, a ring gives equal protection against a cutting blow, and is of course much lighter. The illustration of this form of defensive armour is of rather earlier date than that at which we commence our investigations, but it appears with some frequency in manuscripts of the twelfth century. Mr. J. G. Waller, in his article on the Hauberk of mail in *Archaeologia*, vol. lix, is of opinion that all these arrangements of line represent interlinked chain armour. If this is the case chain-mail must have been much more common than we imagine. From the very nature of its construction and the labour expended on its intricate manufacture it would surely, at least in the earlier periods, have been only the defence of the wealthy. When we examine the protective armour of primitive races we find quilted and studded garments used, even at the present day, so it seems far more probable that our illustrations represent some similar forms of defensive garments than that they are all incompetent renderings of the fabric of chain-mail only.

That the making of chain-mail must have been laborious in the extreme we may judge from the fact that the wire which formed the links had to be hammered out from the solid bar or ingot. As far as can be gathered, the art of wire-drawing was not practised till the fourteenth century, at which time Rudolph of Nuremberg is credited with its discovery. The roughly-hammered strips were probably twisted spirally round an iron or wood core and then cut off into rings of equal size (Fig. 1). The ends of the rings were flattened and pierced, and, when interlaced, the pierced ends were riveted together or sometimes, as is the case with Oriental mail, welded with heat. Links that are ' jumped ', that is with the ends of the ring merely butted together and not joined, generally show either that the mail is an imitation, or that it was

used for some ceremonial purpose ; for this insecure method of
fixing would be useless in the stress and strain of battle or active
service.   The most usual method of interlinking the rings is for
each ring to join four others, as will be seen in the drawing on
Plate I, No. 7.   No. 8 on the same plate shows the mail as
more generally depicted in illuminations.   When we consider the
inexperience of the scribes and illustrators of the Middle Ages we
must admit that this representation of a very intricate fabric
is not only very ingenious but follows quite the best modern
impressionist doctrines.

Portions of chain-mail survive in most armouries and museums,

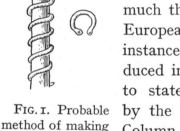

but their provenance is generally unknown, and
much that is of Oriental origin is passed off as
European.   Chain-mail itself comes in the first
instance from the East, but when it was introduced into Europe is difficult, if not impossible,
to state.   It is certainly represented as worn
by the Scythians and Parthians on the Trajan
Column, and is probably of greater antiquity still.

FIG. I. Probable
method of making
links for mail.

From the beginning of the thirteenth century,
for about sixty or seventy years, we find a curious arrangement
of lines intended to represent a form of defensive armour, both
in illuminated manuscripts and also on carved monuments
(Plate I, 12, 13).

Mr. Waller, in the article on the Hauberk referred to above,
gives it as his opinion that this ' Banded Mail ', as it is called, was
but a variety of the ordinary interlinked mail ; but if we examine
the illuminations of the period we shall find that it is shown side
by side with the representation of what all authorities admit to
be chain-mail.   No. 12 on Plate I shows the arm and leg defences
to be formed of this banded mail, while the head is protected with
the ordinary chain-mail.   We have then to try and discover how
these horizontal bands dividing each row of links in the mail can
be shown in a practical form.   Meyrick vaguely suggests a row
of rings sewn edgeways on the body garment and threaded with

a leather thong (Plate I, 10), with the under fabric caught up between the rows of rings and formed into a piping through which a cord was threaded. This theory has been quoted by Viollet-le-Duc in his *Dictionnaire du Mobilier Français*, by Dr. Wendelin Boeheim in his *Waffenkunde*, and by more recent writers ; but none of these authorities seems to have taken the trouble to test its practicability. The human body being rounded, the tendency of these edge-sewn rings would be to ' gape ' and thus give an opening for the weapon. In addition to this, the number of rings so used would make the weight of the defence, hanging as it did from the shoulders alone, almost insupportable. A third and perhaps the most conclusive of all the arguments against Meyrick's theory is that we frequently find the inside of a banded mail coif shown with the same markings as the outside, which aspect would be impossible if the rings were arranged as he suggests.

From models specially made for this work we find that if leather was used at all it must be after the manner of No. 9 on Plate I. Here the rings are covered with the leather on both sides, so that there is no possibility of their gaping, and, in addition, the leather being pressed against the rings, on the outside by wear and usage and on the inside from the pressure of the body, would show ring-markings on front and back which might be represented in the manner shown in the illustration. The drawback to this theory is not only the weight of such a defence, but also the heat from lack of ventilation. By far the most practical theory put forward is that of Mr. Waller,[1] who gives an illustration of a piece of Oriental mail with leather thongs threaded through each alternate row of rings. This gives a certain solidity to the net-like fabric and yet does not add appreciably to its weight. No. 11 on Plate I shows this arrangement drawn from a model, and when we compare it with the figures below, taking into consideration the difficulty of representing such a fabric, we are forced to admit that this last theory is the most practical. This is especially so in No. 12 ; for the mail covering for the head is probably made in one piece

---

[1] *Archaeologia*, lix.

with that of the arms and legs, but the leather thongs have been omitted on the head and hands to give greater ease of movement.

Before leaving the subject of fabrics it may be well to warn those who consult Meyrick that this author is rather prone to enunciate theories of the different forms of mail which, like that of the banded mail, do not work well in practice. He mentions, among many other varieties, what he calls ' Mascled ' mail. He asserts that this was formed of lozenge-shaped plates cut out in the centre and applied to linen or leather. He says that it was so called from its likeness to the meshes of a net (Lat. *macula*). Now when we consider that the word ' mail ' itself comes to us from the Latin ' macula ', through the French ' maille ' and the Italian ' maglia ', we find that Meyrick's ' Mascled mail ' is but a tautological expression which can best be applied to the net-like fabric of the interlinked chain defence, and so his ' Mascled mail ' would more correctly be styled a ' Mascled coat ', and this coat would probably be formed of the chain variety as resembling the meshes of a net more closely than any other fabric.

Double mail is sometimes to be met with on carved monuments, and this would be constructed in the same manner as the single mail ; but two links would be used together in every case where one is used in the single mail.

Having briefly described the varieties of fabric and material which were in use at the time of the Conquest for defensive armour, we may pass to the forms in which those materials were made up. The first garment put on by the man-at-arms was the Tunic, which was a short linen shirt reaching usually to just above the knee ; it is often shown in miniatures of the period beneath the edge of the coat of mail.

At one period the tunic appears to have been worn inconveniently long, if we are to judge from the seals of Richard I, in which it is shown reaching to the feet. This long under-garment was quite given up by the beginning of the thirteenth century, and those representations of Joan of Arc which show a long under-tunic falling from beneath the breastplate are based upon no reliable authority.

Next to the tunic was worn the Gambeson, called also the Wambais and Aketon, a quilted garment, either used as the sole defence by the foot-soldier, or, by the knight, worn under the hauberk to prevent the chain-mail from bruising the body under the impact of a blow. The gambeson is shown on Fig. 9, appearing beneath the edge of the hauberk just above the knee.

The Hauberk, which was worn over the gambeson, was the chief body defence. It is true that we read of a ' plastron de fer ', which seems to have been a solid metal plate worn over the breast and sometimes at the back ; but it was invariably put on either under the hauberk itself or over the hauberk, but always beneath the Jupon or surcoat, which at this period was the outermost garment worn. In either case it was not exposed to view, so it is impossible to tell with any degree of accuracy what was its shape or how it was fixed to the wearer. Hewitt [1] gives two illustrations of carved wooden figures in Bamberg Cathedral, which show a plastron de fer worn over the jupon, which seems to be studded with metal. The figures were executed about the year 1370. The form of the hauberk, as shown on the Bayeux Tapestry, was of the shirt order (Plate I, 4, 6). It was usually slit to the waist, front and back, for convenience on horseback, and the skirts reached to the knee, thus protecting the upper leg. It is perhaps needless to point out that the extreme weight of mail with its thick padded under-garment made the use of a horse a necessity, for the weight was all borne upon the shoulders, and was not, as is the case with suits of plate, distributed over the limbs and body of the wearer. The sleeves of the hauberk were sometimes short ; sometimes they were long and ended in fingerless mittens of mail. The three varieties of sleeve are shown on Plate I, while the mittens turned back to leave the hand bare appear on the Setvans brass (Plate III, 2).

Wace, the chronicler, seems to suggest different forms of defensive habiliments, for we find mention of a short form of the

[1] *Ancient Armour*, ii. 138.

hauberk, called the Haubergeon. In his *Roman de Rou* he writes
of Duke William at the Battle of Senlac :—

Sun boen haubert fist demander,[1]

while of Bishop Odo he says :—

Un haubergeon aveit vestu
De sor une chemise blanche.

The fact that he mentions the tunic (' chemise blanche ') seems to
imply that it was seen beneath the hem of the haubergeon, which
would not be the case with the long-skirted hauberk. Occasionally
in illuminated manuscripts the hauberk is shown slit at the sides;
but for what purpose it is difficult to imagine, for it would impede
the wearer when walking and would make riding an impossibility.

The defences of the leg, made of mail like the hauberk, seem
to have been used, at first, only by the nobles, if the Bayeux
Tapestry is taken as a guide. The common soldiers wore linen or
leather swathings, sometimes studded with metal, but in appearance closely resembling the modern puttee. The upper portion
of the leg was protected at a later period with Chaussons, while the
defences from knee to foot were called Chausses. Wace mentions
' chauces de fer ', but we must remember, as was noticed in the
introduction, that Wace wrote some seventy years after the
Conquest, and probably described the accoutrements worn at his
own time. The Bayeux Tapestry is nearer the period, as far as we
can date it with any correctness, but here we are hampered to
some extent by the crude methods of the embroideress. The
chaussons are not often shown in illuminations, for the long-
skirted hauberk covers the leg to the knee ; but the chausses
appear in all pictorial and sculptured records of the period, made
either of mail or of pourpointerie, that is fabric studded with metal.
Towards the end of the thirteenth century the chaussons and
chausses were made in one stocking-like form covering the foot ; this
is shown on Plate I, 8, 12. In the first of these illustrations only
the front of the leg is covered, and the chausses are laced at the back.

[1] *Roman de Rou*, l. 13254 et seq.

As the manufacture of mail progressed the whole of the wearer's person came to be protected by it. In addition to the coverings of the body we find continuations that protected arms and legs, and in course of time the neck and head were protected with a Coif or hood of mail, which is shown in use in Plate I, No. 12, and thrown back on the shoulders on No. 8. Although of no protective use, the Surcoat is so essentially part of the war equipment of the knight that it needs more than a passing notice. It first appears on Royal seals at the beginning of the thirteenth century, in the reign of King John. Some modern writers have suggested that it was first used in the Crusades to keep the sun off the mail; however this may be, we have written proof that it was of use in protecting the intricate fabric of chain armour from the wet, which by rusting the metal played havoc with its serviceability. It will be seen in different lengths in the figures on Plate I. In *The Avow-ynge of King Arthur*, stanza 39, we find—

> With scharpe weppun and schene
> Gay gowns of grene,
> To hold thayre armur clene
> And were[1] hitte fro the wete.

Like the hauberk, the surcoat was slit to the waist in front and behind for convenience on horseback, and was usually girt at the waist with a cord or belt. It was frequently decorated with the armorial bearings of the wearer. When the barrel helm was worn, concealing the whole face, some such cognizance was necessary that the knight might be recognized. The Setvans brass (Plate III) shows the armorial device powdered over the surcoat.

The headpiece characteristic of the Norman Conquest is the conical nasal Helm. We should draw a distinction between the Helmet and the Helm. The former is, of course, a diminutive of the latter. At the time of the Norman Conquest the head covering would rank rather as a helmet, as it did not entirely cover the face. The Norman helmet was conical, usually formed of four triangular pieces of metal plate riveted in a ring and

---

[1] Protect.

meeting at the apex. Sometimes a Nasal or nose-guard was added (Plate I, 4, 6). That this nasal must have been broad enough to conceal the face to a great extent we may judge from the story how the Norman soldiers believed their leader to be killed, and how William, raising his helm, rode along the

FIG. 2. From the effigy of Hugo Fitz Eudo, Kirkstead, Lincs., thirteenth century.

FIG. 3. From a figure in the Cathedral at Constance, thirteenth century.

lines crying 'I am here, and by God's help I shall conquer'. The Bayeux Tapestry illustrates this incident. On some of the Conqueror's seals we find the helmet tied on with laces. Ear-flaps were sometimes added, as may be seen on the chessmen found in the Isle of Lewis, now in the British Museum.

FIG. 4. From the Great Seal of Alexander II of Scotland, thirteenth century.

FIG. 5. Brit. Mus. Roy. MS. 20. D. i, thirteenth century.

During the twelfth century the helmet gradually became the helm. The ear-flaps were fixed, becoming an integral part of the defence, and closed round to join the nasal, this arrangement forming at length the ventail or visor. This gives us what is known as the 'Barrel helm' (Fig. 2), in which the whole head is enclosed and the only opening in the front is the 'ocularium' or vision slit. Next we have the same kind of helm with the addition of holes for breathing in the lower portion (Fig. 3). In some varieties the back of the helm is shorter than the front, as on Fig. 4, and in this kind also we sometimes find breathing holes added. The Great Seals of the kings are a most useful guide in discovering the accoutrements of each period, and especially so for the helms and helmets, which are easier to distinguish than the more minute details of dress and equipment. It will be understood that in time the flat-topped helm was given up in favour of the 'Sugar-loaf' helm (Fig. 5), as it is generally called, when we consider the importance of a 'glancing surface' in armour. Although thickness of material was of some importance in defensive armour, this providing of surfaces from which a weapon would slip was considered to be of supreme importance by the armour-smiths of later periods. In the conical helm, as indeed in nearly all great helms, the vision and breathing apertures were pierced in the plates of the helm itself and were not part of a movable visor, as was the case in the helmet. The weight of these helms must have been great ; for they do not seem to have been bolted on to the shoulders, as were the fifteenth and sixteenth century tilting helms, but to have rested upon the crown of the head. The drawing on Plate I, No. 8, shows a padded cap which was worn under the mail to protect the head from pressure. On No. 12 of the same plate we see the helm being put on over the mail coif ; the padded cap is worn under the mail. For tournaments the helm was sometimes made of toughened leather, which was called 'cuirbouilli' from the fact that it was prepared by being boiled in oil and then moulded to shape. This material was very strong and serviceable and was used, as we shall see later on, for reinforcing the chain armour and also for horse armour. It was generally decorated with gilding and painting. For the tournament held at Windsor in 1278 we find mention of ' xxxviii galee de cor '.[1] As we have shown, these great helms were not attached to the body armour and were thus liable to be struck off in battle. In order to recover them a chain was sometimes stapled to the helm and fastened to the waist or some portion of the body armour (Fig. 6).

[1] *Archaeologia*, xvii.

The usual form of helmet in the twelfth century is the cup-shaped headpiece of which the Cervellière is a typical example (Fig. 7). It was either worn as the sole defence or was used in conjunction with the helm as an under-cap. The wide-rimmed hat of iron is found all through the period of defensive armour with which we deal. It appears in the thirteenth century (Fig. 8) and is also to be found in the fifteenth. There is an example of one of these war-hats (*Eisenhut*) in the museum at Nuremberg.

FIG. 6. Detail from the brass of Sir Roger de Trumpington, Trumpington, Camb., 1290.

FIG. 7. From the monument to Johan le Botiler, St. Bride's, Glamorganshire, 1300.

FIG. 8. Add. MS. 11. 639, f. 520, thirteenth century.

The Shield at the time of the Conquest was kite-shaped. It was long enough to cover the body and legs of the warrior when mounted, but it must have been a most inconvenient adjunct to his accoutrements. As we have seen in the Monk of St. Gall's records, the shield was sometimes made of iron; but the more usual material was wood covered with leather or the tough cuir-bouilli. Its broad flat surface was from the earliest times used by the painter to display his art, which at first was not systema-tized, but consisted of geometrical patterns and strange birds and beasts that had no special meaning. As time went on each knight retained the device which was borne upon his shield and came to be recognized by it, and from this sprung the complicated science of

Heraldry, which has survived, with all its intricate detail, to the present day. The surface of the shield was often bowed so that it embraced the body of the wearer. That some must have been flat we may suppose from the fact that the soldiers in the Bayeux Tapestry are represented as using them for trays to carry cups and plates at the ' Prandium '. In St. Lucy's Chapel, at Christ Church Cathedral in Oxford, in the window depicting the martyrdom of St. Thomas of Canterbury, are to be seen two

FIG. 9. From the *Romance of Alexander*,   FIG. 10. A, A. Enarmes.
f. 150, Bod. Lib., fourteenth century.   B. Guige.

varieties of decorated shields. Two of the knights bear shields painted with geometrical designs, while Fitz Urse carries a shield on which are three bears' heads erased, a punning cognizance from the name of the wearer. The date of the window is about the end of the thirteenth century. The shield was attached to the wearer by a thong passing round the neck, called the Guige. When not in use it was slung by this thong on the back. When in use the arm and hand passed through the short loops called Enarmes (Fig. 10). The Royal blazon first appears on the shield in the reign of Richard I. Occasionally we find circular shields depicted in illuminations; but they were generally used by the foot-soldiers. As the development of defensive armour proceeds we shall find that the shield becomes smaller, and in time is discarded, the body defences being made sufficient protection in themselves.

CHAPTER II

THE TRANSITION PERIOD (1277–1410)

IT will be readily understood that the change from mail to plate armour was not brought about at once. Difficulty of manufacture, expense, and conservatism in idea, all retarded the innovation. Some progressive knight might adopt a new fashion which did not come into general use till many years after, in the same manner that, from force of circumstances, or from a clinging to old methods, we find an out-of-date detail of armour like the coif of mail, shown on the brass of Sir W. Molineux, appearing in 1548, or the sleeved hauberk in the Dresden Museum which was worn without plate defences for the arms by Herzog August at the Battle of Mühlberg in 1546. Acting on the method adopted in the preceding chapter, we may first consider the materials used during the beginning of the Transition Period, and afterwards we shall show how those materials were made up.

During the fourteenth century iron, leather, whalebone, and quilted fabrics were all employed for defensive purposes. The illustration from the *Romance of Alexander* (Fig. 9) shows the gambeson still worn under the mail, and the legs are covered in one instance with a metal-studded or pourpointed defence ; a second figure wears what appears to be scale armour, while the third has no detail shown upon the legs, which may be an oversight on the part of the artist, or may suggest that plain hose were worn. Iron was used for the mail and scale armour and was also employed in making a pliable defence called Splinted armour, which at a later period became the Brigandine (Plate II).

There are several of these brigandines to be found in the Armouries of England and Europe, but the majority of them date about the middle of the fifteenth century. As will be seen in the

PLATE II

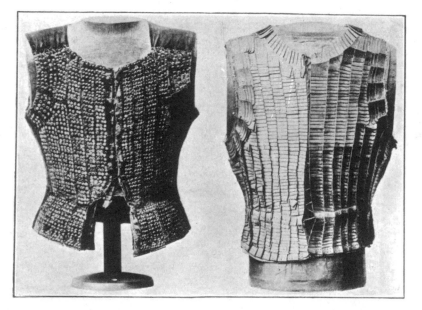

(Outside.)   (Inside.)

Brigandine in the Musée d'Artillerie, Paris.

illustration, the brigandine was made of small plates of iron or steel overlapping upwards and riveted on to a canvas-lined garment of silk or velvet. The plates were worn on the inside in most cases, and the rivet heads which showed on the silk or velvet face were often gilded, thus producing a very brilliant effect.

We find many references to these splinted defences in the Inventories of the period, which form a valuable source of information on the subject of details of armour. The Inventory of Humphrey de Bohun,[1] Earl of Hereford, taken in 1322, gives :—' Une peire de plates coverts de vert velvet.' Again, in one of the Inventories of the Exchequer, 1331,[2] is noted:—' Une peire de plates covert de rouge samyt.' The Inventory of Piers Gaveston, dated 1313, a document full of interesting details, has [3] :—' Une peire de plates enclouez et garniz d'argent.' The ' pair of plates ' mentioned in these records refers to the front and back defences. In the accounts of payments by Sir John Howard we find in the year 1465, 11s. 8d. paid for 20,000 ' Bregander nayles '.[4] Brass was employed for decorative purposes on the edges of the hauberk, or was fashioned into gauntlets, as may be seen in the gauntlets of the Black Prince, preserved at Canterbury: Chaucer writes in the ' Rime of Sir Thopas ' :—

> His swerdes shethe of yvory,
> His helm of laton bright.

Laton, or latten, was a mixed metal, much resembling brass, used at this period for decorative purposes.

Whalebone was employed for gauntlets and also for swords used in the tournament. Froissart uses the words ' gands de baleine ' in describing the equipment of the troops of Philip von Arteveld at the Battle of Rosbecque.

Quilted garments were still worn, either as the sole defence or as a gambeson under the mail. As late as the year 1460 we find

---

[1] *Arch. Journ.*, ii. 349.
[2] Vol. iii. p. 165.
[3] *New Foedera*, ii. 203.
[4] *Arch. Journ.*, lx. 95–136.

regulations of Louis XI of France ordering these coats of defence to be made of from 30 to 36 folds of linen.[1]

Leather, either in its natural state or boiled and beaten till it could be moulded and then allowed to dry hard, was frequently used at this period for all kinds of defensive armour.

In Chaucer's ' Rime of Sir Thopas ', from which we have quoted before, occur the words, ' His jambeux were of quirboilly.' The jambeaux were coverings for the legs. This quirboilly, cuirbully, or cuirbouilli, when finished was an exceedingly hard substance, and was, on account of its lightness as compared to metal, much used for tournament armour and for the Barding or defence for the horse. In the Roll of Purchases for the Windsor Park Tournament, held in 1278, mention is made of cuirasses supplied by Milo the Currier, who also furnished helms of the same material.[2] In the Inventory of Sir Simon Burley, beheaded in 1338, we find under ' Armure de guerre ' :—' Un palet (a headpiece) de quierboylle.' There is a light leather helmet of the ' morion ' type, dated sixteenth century, in the Zeughaus at Berlin.

Banded mail still appears in drawings or on monuments up to the end of the fourteenth century.

We may now turn to the making up of these varied materials, and will endeavour, step by step, to trace the gradual evolution of the full suit of plate from the first additions of plate defence to mail till we find that the mail practically disappears, or is only worn in small portions where plate cannot be used.

Setting aside the plastron de fer, which, as has been noticed, is seldom shown in representations of armour, we find the first additional defence was the Poleyne or knee-cop. We must suppose that there was good reason for thus reinforcing the mail defence on this part of the body. Probably this was due to the fact that the shield became shorter at this period, and also because the position of the wearer when mounted exposed the knee, a very delicate piece of anatomy, to the attacks of the foot-soldier (Fig. 11). Poleynes are mentioned in a wardrobe account of Edward I in

---

[1] *Arch. Journ.*, lx. 95–136.   [2] *Archaeologia*, xvii.

1300. They were frequently made of cuirbouilli, and this material is probably intended in the illustration (Plate III, 1), as elaborately decorated metal is rarely met with at this period. At the end of the thirteenth century appear those curious appendages known as Ailettes. On Plate III, 2, the figure is shown wearing the poleynes and also the ailettes. For practical purposes they are represented on recumbent figures as worn at the back, but in pictorial illustrations they are invariably shown on the outside of the shoulder.

FIG. 11. From Roy. MS. 16. G. vi, f. 387, fourteenth century.

FIG. 12. Bib. Nat., Paris, *Lancelot du Lac*, fourteenth century.

Some writers consider that they were solely used for ornament, presumably because they are generally shown decorated with heraldic blazons. Against this, however, we may place the fact that they are depicted in representations of battles, and in Queen Mary's psalter (2. B. vii in the British Museum) the combatants wear plain ailettes. The German name for the ailettes (*Tartschen*) suggests also that they were intended for shoulder-guards. Fourteenth-century Inventories abound with references to ailettes. In the Roll of Purchases for Windsor Park Tournament are mentioned thirty-eight pair of ailettes to be fastened with silk laces supplied by one Richard Paternoster. In the Piers Gaveston Inventory before quoted are: 'Les alettes garnis et frettez de perles.' These, of course, would be only for ceremonial use. The illustration (Fig. 11) shows different forms of ailette, and occasionally we find the lozenge-shaped, and once (Brit. Mus. Roy. MS. 2. A. xxii, fol. 219) they assume a cruciform shape. The attachment of the ailettes with the laces referred to in the Windsor Park Inventory is shown on Fig. 12. In the *Chroniques de Charlemaine*, preserved in the Bibliothèque Royale at Brussels, the ailettes appear to be laced to the side of the helmet. This occurs in so many of the miniatures that it must be taken as a correct presentment of this detail in arming. It may be, however, that, as this manuscript was produced in the year 1460, it recorded a later method of using the ailette which, *per se*, disappears about the middle of the fourteenth century, as far as monumental records exist.

The next addition of plate to the equipment of mail seems to have been on the legs. The only monumental brass that gives this fashion of arming is the Northwode brass at Minster, Sheppey. As the legs are of later date than the rest of the brass, although most probably correct in design, it may be better to trust to a monument which is intact, as is the statue of Gulielmus Berardi, 1289, which is carved in the Cloister of the Annunziata Convent, Florence (Fig. 13). Here we find the front of the leg entirely protected by plates which may be intended for metal, but which, from their ornate decoration, seem rather to suggest cuirbouilli. These jambeaux, or, as they are sometimes called, Bainbergs or Beinbergs, of leather have been before referred to as mentioned by Chaucer.

Returning to monumental brasses again, we find on the Gorleston brass (Plate III, 3) that the plate additions are still more increased. Besides the poleynes and the ailettes there are traces of plate jambs on the legs, and the arms are protected by plates and circular discs on shoulder and elbow.

After 1325 ailettes are rarely met with. On No. 4 of Plate III these details seem to be advanced in some points, and are shown with the methods of attaching them to the wearer. The Rerebrace is strapped over the mail, and the disc at the bend of the Coude

PLATE III

1. Sir John d'Aubernoun, 1277, Stoke D'Abernon, Surrey 2. Sir Robt. de Setvans, 1306, Chartham, ~ Kent 3. A member of the de Bacon family, c.1320, Gorleston, Suffolk 4. Sir John D'Aubernoun, 1327, Stoke D'Abernon, Surrey 5. William de Aldeburgh, c.1360, Aldborough, Yorks 6. A Knight, c.1400, Laughton, Lincolnshire.

or elbow-piece is held in place by Aiguillettes or laces—called at a later period Arming-points. The poleynes overlap the jambs, and so cover the junction of the two pieces, and the latter are held to the leg with straps. The Solerets are among the earliest examples of a defence of laminated plates, that is, of strips of metal riveted upon leather in order to give more ease of movement than would be possible with a solid plate. The Vambrace is worn under the sleeve of the hauberk, and not, as in the preceding example,

FIG. 13.   Gulielmus Berardi,
Florence, 1289.

FIG. 14.   Bib. Nat., Paris, *Tristan and Iseult*, fourteenth century.

over the mail. This figure is especially interesting because it shows the different garments worn with the armour of this period. Above the knees appears the tunic; over this comes the hauberk of mail, in this instance banded mail; over the hauberk are shown the Upper Pourpoint, a quilted garment, and, above this, the surcoat, or, as this variety is called, the Cyclas. The difference between the surcoat proper and the cyclas is that the former is of even length all round, while the latter is shorter in front than behind (see also Fig. 14). The coif of mail has now given place to the Camail, which does not cover the head, but is attached to the helmet, and is not joined to the hauberk, but hangs over the cyclas.

In the next example (Plate III, 5) we find the mail still worn on the legs and arms, but on the latter the vambrace and the coude plate seem to be hinged in the manner adopted during the period of full armour. The upper part of the leg is protected by studded pourpointerie, which was frequently employed as being of more convenience on horseback. These thigh defences were called the Cuisses. The Bascinet is shown and also the short surcoat or Jupon.

The brass of an unknown knight (Plate III, 6) is typical of what has come to be known as the 'Camail' period. The arm- and leg-pieces completely enclose the limb and are fastened with hinges and straps as in the later periods. The gauntlets show the Gadlings, or knuckle-knobs, which are a marked feature of this period, and the whole suit is richly decorated with engraved borders. Some writers divide the Transition Period of armour into 'Surcoat', 'Cyclas', 'Jupon', and 'Tabard'. This, however, seems unnecessary if we are considering only the development of defensive armour, and not the whole question of costume. The camail is so marked a detail of the knightly equipment that it may reasonably be used to describe the fashion in armour from about 1360 to 1405. In this example the figure is clad in complete plate, though the hauberk is worn beneath, as may be seen at the lower edge of the jupon and also in the ' vif de l'harnois ', or portion of the body at the armpit, which was unprotected by plate. In some instances this vital spot was protected by a circular, oval, crescent-shaped, or square plate attached by laces, which modern writers call the Rondel, but which Viscount Dillon, in a most interesting article, proves to have been the Moton or Besague [1] (Fig. 15).

The effigy of the Black Prince at Canterbury is a good example of the armour of this period, but it is interesting to note that, while the monumental brasses frequently give such details as straps, buckles, &c., this effigy shows no constructional detail whatever. We find that in Spain there were minute regulations drawn up as to the manner in which a deceased warrior might be represented on his tomb. The details of sheathed or unsheathed sword, helm,

[1] *Arch. Journ.*, lxiv. 15–23.

spurs, &c., all had some significant reference to his life and achievements.[1] It is almost superfluous to point out that those details which referred to the knight's captivity, or the fact that he had been vanquished, were more honoured in the breach than in the observance.

The armour of this period was often richly decorated with engraving, as may be seen on the brass to an unknown knight

FIG. 16. Knightly figure in Ash Church, Kent, fourteenth century.

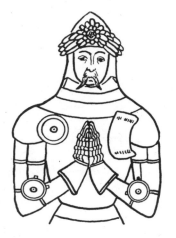

FIG. 15. Brass of Sir T. de S. Quentin, Harpham, Yorks, 1420.

FIG. 17. Bib. Nat., Paris, *Tite-Live*, 1350.

at Laughton, Lincs., and also on the monument to Sir Hugh Calverley at Bunbury, Cheshire. Of the jupon, King René, in his *Livre des Tournois*, about the year 1450, writes that it ought to be without fold on the body, like that of a herald, so that the cognizance, or heraldic blazon, could be better recognized. The jupon of the Black Prince, preserved at Canterbury and admirably figured in *Monumenta Vetusta*, vol. vii, is embroidered with the Royal Arms, and is quilted with cotton padding. So general is the use of the jupon at this period that it is a matter of some conjecture

[1] Carderera, *Iconografia.*

as to what form the body armour took that was worn under it. The effigy of a knight in Ash Church, Kent (Fig. 16), elucidates this mystery and shows, through openings of the jupon, horizontal plates or splints riveted together. In Fig. 17 we see these plates worn without the jupon. The term Jazeran is often applied to such armour.

The camail, or hood of mail, which we have before referred to, was separate from the hauberk, and during the fourteenth century was worn over the jupon. It was attached to the bascinet by Vervelles or staples which fitted into openings in the helmet. A lace was passed through these staples, as is shown on Fig. 18.

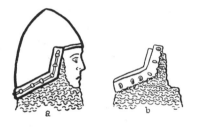

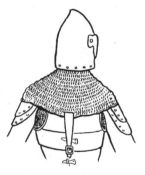

FIG. 18. *a.* The Camail attached to the helm.
    b. The Camail showing the staples.

FIG. 19. Bib. Nat., Paris,
    Tite-Live, 1350.

From a French manuscript of the early fifteenth century (Fig. 19) we see how the camail was kept from ' riding ' over the shoulders. In the little wooden statuette of St. George of Dijon, which is a most useful record of the armour of this period, we find that, in addition, the camail is fastened to the breast with aiguillettes.

The Great Heaume, or helm, of the fourteenth century differs but little from those of the late thirteenth century which were noticed in a preceding chapter. The shape was either of the sugar-loaf order or a cylinder surmounted by a truncated cone (Fig. 20). Notable examples of actual specimens in England at the present day are the helms of Sir Richard Pembridge at Hereford Cathedral and the helm of the Black Prince, surmounted by a crest of wood and cuirbouilli, preserved at Canterbury. In an Inventory of Louis Hutin, made in 1316, we find: 'ii heaummes d'acier, item v autres dans li uns est dorez.' This seems to suggest that the gilded helm was of some other material than steel, possibly leather. It is rare to come across constructional detail in illuminations, but the illustration (Fig. 21) from a French manuscript of about the year 1350 shows a method of attaching the helm to the wearer's body. In the preceding chapter we noticed the chain used for this purpose on the Trumpington brass.

FIG. 20.   Fourteenth-century helm,   FIG. 21.   Bib. Nat., Paris,
Zeughaus, Berlin.   Tite-Live, 1350.

The most popular of the light helmets at this period was the Bascinet. It appears on nearly every monumental brass that depicts a military figure, and is an essential part of that style of equipment known as the 'camail'. The later form of bascinet has a movable visor which is known among armour collectors as the 'pig-faced' bascinet (Plate V). Sometimes the hinge is at the top, and sometimes, as in No. 2 of this plate, the visor is pivoted at the sides. Froissart calls the visor 'carnet' and 'visière'. In the Bohun Inventory, before referred to, are given: 'ii bacynettes, lun covert de quir lautre bourni.' This shows that while some helmets were of polished metal, others were covered with leather, and indeed silk and velvet as fancy dictated. Frequent references to these 'covers' for helmets occur in Inventories and Wills. The helmet and other portions of the suit of plate armour were some-

PLATE IV

Photograph by Hauser & Menet

Jousting armour of Charles V.　Madrid.

times tinned to prevent rust, as is shown in one of the Dover Castle Inventories of 1361 :—' xiii basynetz tinez.' Sometimes, in the case of Royalty or princes of rank, the bascinet was encircled with a fillet or crown of gold and gems. Among the payments of Etienne de Fontaine, in 1352, are mentioned 110 crowns for ' quarente grosses perles pour garnir le courroye du basinet de Monsieur le Dauphin'. The Orle, or wreath worn turban-wise round the bascinet, is sometimes shown, as on Fig. 22, of a decorative nature. It is supposed by some writers to have been devised to take the pressure of the great helm from the head, for the helm was often worn, as in the preceding century, over a lighter headpiece. From the usual position of the orle, however, and from the fact that it is invariably shown highly decorated and jewelled, this explanation can hardly hold good, for a padding worn as shown in the illustration would not be of much service in keeping off the pressure of the helm, and of course the jewelled decoration would be destroyed at once. Another theory is that the orle was made by wrapping the Lambrequin or Mantling—which hung from the back of the helmet and which is still used in heraldic drawings—much in the same manner as the modern puggaree is worn in India. In this illustration appears also the gorget of plate that was worn over the throat and chin with the bascinet.

FIG. 22. The Orle, from the monument of Sir H. Stafford, Bromsgrove, Kent, 1450.

The shields of the fourteenth century present an infinite variety in shape and decoration. The heraldic blazoning has by this time been systematized into somewhat of a science, which in Germany especially was carried to extravagant extremes. The long kite-shaped shield is to be found in records of the period, but the more common forms were the short pointed shield as shown on Plate III, and that which was rounded at the lower edge. Frequently the shield is represented as 'bouché', or notched, at the top right-hand corner, to enable the wearer to point his lance through this opening without exposing his arm or body to attack. In the Inventory of Louis Hutin are mentioned ' iii ecus pains des armes le Roy, et un acier ', which shows that the shield was sometimes made of steel, though usually it was fashioned of wood and faced with leather, or of cuirbouilli. In a transcript of Vegecius (Brit. Mus. Roy. MS. 18. A. xii) the young knight is advised to have ' a shelde of twigges sumewhat rounde '. The shield of the Black Prince at Canterbury is pointed at the lower edge, and is made of wood faced with leather, on which are set out the Royal arms in gesso-duro or plaster relief.

CHAPTER III

THE WEARING OF ARMOUR AND ITS CONSTRUCTIONAL DETAILS

BEFORE proceeding to examine the suit of Full Plate, with all its interesting details and differences as exemplified in the various armouries of England and Europe, it will be well to make clear the main principles which governed the manufacture of such armour. We should remember that the whole history of our subject is one long struggle of defensive equipment against offensive weapons. This is brought out clearly at the present day in the Navy, where the contest between gun and armour-plating is the dominant factor in naval construction. As the weapons of the Middle Ages became more serviceable, the armour was increased in weight. The Longbow and the Crossbow marked distinct periods in the development of defensive armour ; for so important a factor did these weapons become, especially the latter, that they were used for testing the temper of the metal, large or small weapons being used as occasion demanded. Those writers who are prone to generalize upon such subjects tell us that the invention of gunpowder sounded the knell of defensive armour, but this is by no means accurate, for guns were used in sieges as early as 1382, and, as we shall find farther on in this chapter, the armour of the late sixteenth century was proved by pistol shot. The result of the improvement of firearms was that for many years armour became heavier and thicker till the musket was perfected, and then it was found that even highly-tempered steel would not resist the impact of a bullet.

It is a safe assertion to make that a full suit of plate armour at its finest period—the fifteenth century—is the most perfect work of craftsmanship that exists.

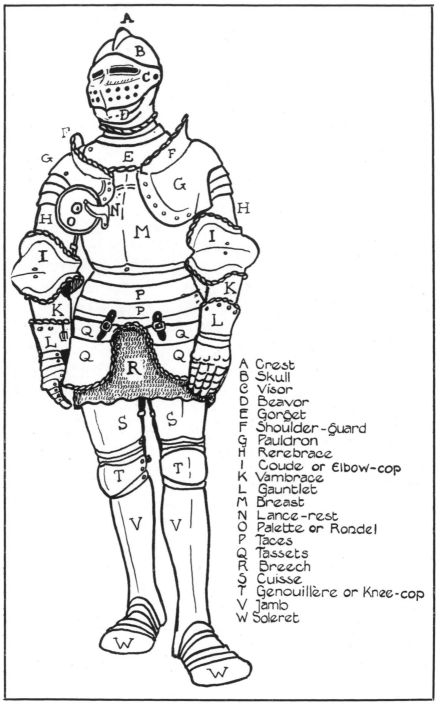

A Crest
B Skull
C Visor
D Beavor
E Gorget
F Shoulder-guard
G Pauldron
H Rerebrace
I Coude or Elbow-cop
K Vambrace
L Gauntlet
M Breast
N Lance-rest
O Palette or Rondel
P Taces
Q Tassets
R Breech
S Cuisse
T Genouillère or Knee-cop
V Jamb
W Soleret

FIG. 23.

This assertion is not made without fully considering the real value of such work, which must fulfil all those essentials without which no true work of craftsmanship can have any merit. The first of these is that the work should fulfil its object in the best possible manner ; secondly, that it should be convenient and simple in use ; thirdly, that it should proclaim its material ; and fourthly, and this is by no means the least important, that any decoration should be subservient to its purpose. To take our axioms in the order given, it may appear to the casual student that if armour were sufficiently thick it would naturally fulfil its

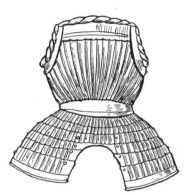

FIG. 24. Maximilian breastplate and taces.   FIG. 25. Coude or Elbow-cop.

primary reason for existence. But we find, on careful examination of plate armour, that there are other considerations which are of equal, if not greater importance. Of these the most noticeable is the 'glancing surface'. It is somewhat difficult to exemplify this by a line-drawing, though it is easy to do so with an actual example. Referring to the Maximilian breastplate (Fig. 24), we find that a lance, the thrusting weapon much favoured in the fifteenth and sixteenth centuries, would, on striking the breast be deflected along the grooved channel nearest to the point of impact till it reached the raised edge either at the top or at the sides, when it would be conducted safely off the body of the wearer. The same surface is to be noticed on all helms and helmets after the twelfth century, the rounded surfaces giving no sure hold for cutting or thrusting weapons. The Coude (Fig. 25) shows this same glancing surface used to protect the elbow, and, again, the fan-shaped plate on the outside of the knee effects the same result (see Frontispiece).[1] The great jousting helms are so constructed that the lance-point should glance off them when the wearer is in the proper jousting position, that is, bent forward at such an angle that the eyes come on a level with the ocularium or vision slit (Plate V, 5). These helms are also made of plates varying in thickness as the part may be more exposed to attack. The Great Helm in the possession of Captain Lindsay of Sutton Courtenay, near Abingdon, has a skull-plate nearly a quarter of an inch thick, for, in the bending position adopted by the wearer, this portion of the helm would be most exposed to the lance. The back-plate is less than half that thickness. This helm is one of the heaviest in existence, for it weighs 25 lb. 14 oz. Again, we may notice the overlapping Lames or strips of steel that are so frequently used for Pauldron, Rerebrace, Vambrace, Soleret, and Gauntlet; all present the same surface to the opposing weapon, and, except in the case of the Taces, where the overlapping from necessity of form must be in an inverse direction, the chance of a weapon penetrating the joints is reduced to a minimum (Fig. 23). A portion of the pauldron which is designed for this glancing defence, and for this only, is the upstanding Neck- or Shoulder-guard which is so generally described as the Passe-guard. It is curious, with the very definite information to hand (supplied by Viscount Dillon in the *Archaeological Journal*, vol. xlvi, p. 129), that even the most recent writers fall into the same mistake about the name of this defence. Space will not admit of quoting more fully Viscount Dillon's interesting paper; but two facts cited by him prove conclusively that the

---

[1] The terms 'coude' and 'genouillière', 'palette,' and such-like words of French origin, are open to some objection in an English work when 'elbow-cop', 'knee-cop', or 'poleyne' and 'rondel' can be substituted. They are only employed here because of their general use in armouries at the present day, and because the English words are of rarer occurrence and are less likely to be met with by those beginning the study of armour. 'Cuisse' and 'cuissard', however, are always used for the thigh-pieces, and no anglicized term is found in contemporary writings unless it be 'Quysshews.'

PLATE V

1. Bascinet from the tomb of the Black Prince, Canterbury, XIVth. cent. ～～
2. Visored Bascinet from the statuette of S. George, Dijon, XIVth. cent. ～～
3. Salade, Royal Armoury, Turin, XVth. cent   4. Salade with visor and beavor ～
Musée de la porte de Hal, Brussels, XVth. cent   5. The Brocas Helm, Rotunda
Woolwich XVth.-XVIth. cent   6. Armet, Royal Armoury, Turin   7. Burgonet,～
Brit. Mus. XVIth. cent   8. Burgonet and Buffe, Royal Armoury, Turin XVIth.cent
9. Morion, Brussels, XVIth. cent.   10. Cabasset, Turin, XVIth. cent   11. Lobster-
tailed Pot helmet, Turin, XVIIth. cent.

passe-guard is quite another portion of the armour. In the Tower Inventory of 1697 appears the entry, ' One Armour cap-a-pe Engraven with a Ragged Staffe, made for ye Earle of Leisester, a Mainfere, Passguard and Maineguard and Gantlett.' Now it is hardly reasonable to suppose that this ridge on the pauldron should be specially mentioned as the Passe-guard without any notice of the pauldron itself. In the Additional Notes to the above article Viscount Dillon gives, from a List of Payments made in connexion with jousts held on October 20, 1519, ' 9 yards of Cheshire cotton at 7d. for lining the king's pasguard.'   That the neck-guard to which we refer should need lining on the inside, where it did not even touch the helmet, we may dismiss at once ; and that the lining should be on the outside is of course absurd. As far as can be gathered from recent research the passe-guard is a reinforcing piece for the right elbow, used for jousting. It was lined to protect the ordinary arm defence underneath from being scratched, and also to lessen the shock to the wearer if it were struck.   It is to be hoped, from this reiteration of Viscount Dillon's researches, that at any rate one of the many errors of nomenclature in armour may be corrected.

With regard to the thickness of plate armour, we should remember that it was forged from the solid ingot, and was not rolled in sheets as is the material of to-day from which so many forgeries are manufactured. The armourer was therefore able to graduate the thickness of his material, increasing it where it was most needed, and lessening it in those parts which were less exposed.

With regard to the proving of armour an article in *Archaeologia*, vol. li, also by Viscount Dillon, is of great interest as showing the indifferent skill of the English ironsmiths of the sixteenth century. In 1590 a discussion arose as to the quality of the English iron found in Shropshire as compared to the ' Hungere ' iron which came from Innsbruck. After some delay Sir Henry Lee, Master of the Tower Armouries, arranged a test, and two breastplates were prepared, of equal make and weight. Two pistol charges of equal power were fired at the test breastplates, with the result

PLATE VI

[*Photograph by Viscount Dillon.*

Engraved suit of armour given to Henry VIII by the Emperor Maximilian.
Tower.

that the foreign armour was only slightly dented, while the English plate was pierced completely, and the beam on which it rested was torn by the bullet. A bascinet in the Tower, which belonged to Henry VIII, bears two indented marks, signifying that it was proof against the large crossbow. In the Musée d'Artillerie in Paris, a suit made for Louis XIV bears proof marks which are treated as the centres for floriated designs (Plate VIII). No excuse need be offered for thus borrowing from papers by Viscount Dillon and other writers in *Archaeologia* and the *Archaeological Journal*, for these publications are not always at hand to those interested in the subject of armour and equipments. They are, however, indispensable for careful study; for they contain reports of the most recent discoveries and investigations of the subject, and are written, for the most part, by men whose expert knowledge is at once extensive and precise.

Another detail of importance in connexion with the protective power of armour occurs in the great jousting helms, which invariably present a smooth surface on the left side, even when there may be some opening, for ventilation or other purposes, on the right. The reason for this was that the jouster always passed left arm to left arm with the lance pointed across the horse's neck. It was therefore important that there should be no projection or opening on the left side of the helm in which the lance-point could possibly be caught.

We next turn our attention to Convenience in Use. Under this head the armourer had to consider that the human body makes certain movements of the limbs for walking and riding, or fighting with arm and hand. He had so to construct the different portions of the suit that they should allow of all these movements without hindrance; and at the same time he had to endeavour to protect the body and limbs while the movements were taking place. The arrangements for pivoting elbow- and knee-joints need scarcely be detailed; for it will be seen by a glance at any suit of plate armour how the cuisse and jamb are pivoted on to the genouillière, and move with the leg to a straight or bent position

without allowing these plates to escape from under the genouillière.   The coude is sometimes pivoted in the same manner, but
more often it is rigid and of such circumference that the arm can
bend within it and yet be very adequately protected.   In the
overlapping lames or strips of metal which give ease of movement to the upper arm, the hands, the waist, and the foot, we
find that much careful work and calculation was needed to ensure
comfort to the wearer.   On the foot, the toepiece and four or more
arches of metal overlap upwards on to a broader arch, while above
this three or more arches overlap downwards, thus allowing the
toe-joint and ankle to be bent at the same time (Fig. 26).   In
a suit in the Tower, made for Prince Henry, son of James I, all
the arches of the soleret overlap downwards.   This points to
a certain decadence in the craftsmanship of the armourer of the
period, though the excuse might be offered for him that the suit
was intended only for use on horseback.   There are generally one,
two, or more of these movable lames joining the genouillière to
the jamb, and above this the cuisse to the genouillière to give
greater flexibility to the knee fastenings.   The separate arm- and
leg-pieces are, when made in two halves to encircle the limb,
hinged on the outside and closed with strap and buckle, or with
locking hook or bolt on the inside.   This, of course, is to ensure
greater protection to these fastenings, especially on horseback.
Higher up again we get the tuilles or taces, which, from the fact
that to adapt themselves to the human form they must narrow
at the waist and spread out below, overlap upwards.   From
the taces are hung the tassets, with strap and buckle, which
give increased protection to the upper leg, and yet are not in
any way rigid.   When the tassets are made of more than one
plate they are attached to each other by a most ingenious
arrangement of straps and sliding rivets.   On the inner edge of
each plate the rivets are attached to a strap on the under
side ; but the outer edge, requiring more compression of the
lames together, is furnished with rivets fixed firmly in the upper-
most plate and working loose in a slot in the back plate, thus

PLATE VII

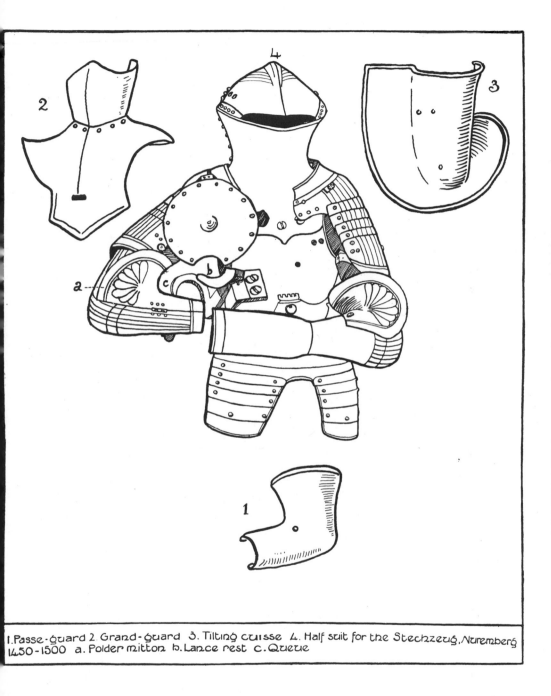

1. Passe-guard 2 Grand-guard 3. Tilting cuisse 4. Half suit for the Stechzeug, Nuremberg 1450-1500 a. Polder mitton b. Lance rest c. Queue

allowing an expansion or contraction of half an inch or more to each lame. It is somewhat difficult to explain this ingenious arrangement in words, but Fig. 27 will show how the straps and rivets are set. When the tassets were discarded about the end of the sixteenth century the cuisses were laminated in this way from waist to knee.

The gauntlet is generally found with a stiff cuff, and from wrist to knuckles the plates in narrow arches overlap towards the arm, where they join a wider plate which underlaps the cuff. The knuckle-plate is usually ridged with a rope-shaped crest or with bosses imitating the knuckles. The fingers are protected by

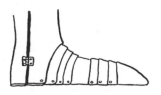

FIG. 26. Soleret.

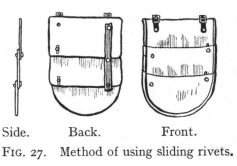

Side.   Back.   Front.

FIG. 27. Method of using sliding rivets.

small plates, from four on the fourth finger to six on the second finger (in some examples there are more or less), which overlap from knuckle to finger-tip. The thumb is covered in like manner, but has a lozenge-shaped plate to connect it to the cuff. This metal hand-covering was sewn on to a leather glove or attached to it with leather loops (Fig. 28). The vambrace is generally rigid, either a solid tube or hinged on the outside and fastened on the inside by straps or hooks. It is held to the lower edge of the coude by a rivet. The lower portion of the rerebrace is also tubular, while the upper portion, where it joins the pauldron, is often laminated, with the plates overlapping, downwards as a rule, though there are instances of these plates overlapping upwards. They are joined in the same way as the laminated tassets by a riveted strap on the inner side, and by sliding rivets at the back, thus giving the arm freedom of movement forwards in the direction most needed, but less freedom towards the back.

These sliding rivets working in slots have come to be called
'Almain' rivets from the fact that the Almain rivet, a light half
suit of armour, was put together to a great extent by this method.
These suits will be referred to later in the chapter.

The Pauldron is hung on the shoulder by a strap from the
gorget or the breastplate, or it is pierced with a hole which fits
over a pin fixed in one of these portions of the armour. In most
suits of plate of the fifteenth and early sixteenth century that
portion of the pauldron which covers the breastplate is larger on

FIG. 29.   Turning 'lock-pins'.

FIG. 28.   Gauntlet.

FIG. 30.   Gorget.

the left side than on the right. The reason for this is that the
position of the lance when held 'in rest', that is couched for the
charge, necessitates a certain curtailment of the front plate of
the pauldron, and, at the same time, the left arm being held rigid
at the bridle, and being exposed to the attacking weapon, requires
more protection than does the right, which, when using the lance,
was guarded by the Vamplate or metal disc fixed to the lance
above the Grip.

Breast- and back-pieces are held together on the shoulders and
sides by straps, but the lames of the taces, and in some cases the
breast and back themselves, are fastened with turning pins which
play an important part in holding the suit together (Fig. 29).

The Gorget (Fig. 30) is made in two halves, each composed of
a single plate or, sometimes, of two or three horizontal lames.
The two portions are united by a loose-working rivet on the left
side and are joined by a turning pin on the right. The gorget was
worn either over or under the breast- and backplates.

Perhaps the most ingeniously contrived suit in existence,
which completely protects the wearer and at the same time
follows the anatomical construction of the human body, is that
made for Henry VIII for fighting on foot in the lists. It is num-
bered xxviii in the Armoury of the Tower. There are no parts
of the body or limbs left uncovered by plate, and every separate
portion fits closely to its neighbour with sliding rivets and turning
pins to give the necessary play for the limbs. It is composed of
235 pieces and weighs 93 lb.

The wearing of the bascinet, salade, burgonet, and like helmets
needs no detailed description. In the preceding chapter we noticed
the method of attaching the camail to the bascinet. When the
great helm was made a fixture in the fifteenth century, as distinct
from the loose or chained helms of preceding periods, it was either
bolted to the breast and back, as on Plate VII, or it was fastened
by an adjustable plate which shut over a locking pin, as shown
on Plate V, 5, and a somewhat similar arrangement at the back,
or a strap and buckle, held it firmly in place, while if extra rigidity
was needed it was supplied by straps from the shoulders to the
lugs shown in the drawing of the Brocas Helm on Plate V. The
Armet, or close helmet, fits the shape of the head to such an extent
that it must be opened to be put on. This is arranged by hingeing
the side plates to the centre, and, when fixed, fastening them with
a screw at the back to which a circular disc is added as a protection
to this fastening (Fig. 31). The armet shown on Plate V opens in
the front and when closed is fastened with a spring hook. The
different parts of the armet are the Ventail, A, and Vue, B, which
together make the Visor ; the Skull, C ; and the Beavor, D
(Plate V, 6).

Having now arrived at some understanding of the construction of the suit of armour we will pass on to the wearing of the suit. A man could not wear his ordinary clothes under his armour ; the friction of the metal was too great. In spite of the excellence of workmanship of the armourer ·any thin substance was bound to be torn, so a strong fabric was chosen which is called in contemporary records Fustian. Whether it at all resembled the modern fabric of that name it is difficult to determine, but certainly the wearing powers of this material or of corduroy would be admirably adapted for the purpose. Chaucer writes in the Prologue to the *Canterbury Tales*, line 75 :

> Of fustyan he wered a gepoun
> Alle bysmoterud with his haburgeoun.

This would refer to the rust-stains that penetrated through the interstices of the mail. In Hall's *Chronicles* (p. 524) is mentioned a levy of troops ordered for the wars in France in 1543, for which it was enjoined: 'Item every man to hav an armyng doublet of ffustyean or canvas ', and also ' a capp to put his scull or sallet in '. These last were coverings for the

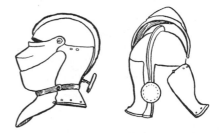

FIG. 31.   Armet.

helmets which we have noted on page 42. The helmets had linings, either riveted to the metal or worn separately as a cap. The tilting helm was provided with a thick padded cap with straps to keep it in its place. Some of these caps exist in the Museum at Vienna.

King René, in his *Livre des Tournois*, advises a pourpoint or padded undergarment to be put on under the body armour, ' stuffed to the thickness of three fingers on the shoulders for there the blows fall heaviest.' It seems that in Brabant and the Low Countries the blows fell heavier, or that the combatants were less hardy, for he advises for them a thickness of four fingers, filled with cotton. Viscount Dillon mentions in his Armour Notes [1] the fact that a ' stuffer of Bacynetts ' accompanied Henry V to

[1] *Arch. Journ.*, lx.

Agincourt. He also quotes a letter from James Croft to Cecil on July 1, 1559, which states that a man cannot keep his corselet and pay for the wear and tear of his clothes due to the rubbing of the body armour, under 8*d.* per day.

Sir John Smith, in his *Animadversions* (1591), writes: 'No man should wear any cut doublets, as well in respect that the wearing of armour doth quickly fret them out, and also by reason that the corners and edges of the lames and joints of the armour do take such hold upon such cuttes as they do hinder the quick and sudden arming of men.'

An interesting description of the arming of a man, entitled, '*Howe a manne schall be armed at hys ese when he schall fighte on foote,*' is preserved in the *Life of Sir John Astley* (a manuscript in the possession of Lord Hastings).[1] The knight is first dressed in a doublet of fustian, lined with satin, which is cut with holes for ventilation. This satin was to keep the roughness of the fustian from the wearer's body ; for he wore no shirt under it. The doublet was provided with gussets of mail, or Vuyders, attached under the armpit and at the bend of the elbow by Arming Points or laces. These mail gussets were to protect the parts not covered by the plate armour. The 'Portrait of an Italian Nobleman' by Moroni, in the National Gallery, shows the figure dressed in this arming doublet. A pair of thick worsted hose were worn, and shoes of stout leather. It must be noticed here that the soleret, or sabaton as it is sometimes called, covered only the top of the foot, and had understraps which kept it to the sole of the shoe. First the sabatons were put on, then the jambs, genouillière and cuisses, then the skirt or breech of mail round the waist. This is sometimes known as the Brayette. Then the breast- and backplates were buckled on with the accompanying taces, tassets, and Garde-rein or plates to protect the loins. After this the arm defences, and, if worn over the breastpiece, the gorget ; and, finally, the helmet completed the equipment. The sword was buckled on the left side and the dagger on the right.

[1] *Archaeologia*, vol. lvii; *Arch. Journ.*, vol. iv.

The armour for jousts and tourneys was much heavier than the Hosting or War harness. From the fact, which has been previously noticed, that the combatants passed each other on the left, this side of the armour was reinforced to such a degree that in time it presented a totally different appearance from the right side (see Plate VII). The weight of jousting armour was so great that it was impossible for the wearer to mount without assistance. De Pluvinel, in his *Maneige Royal* (1629), gives an imaginary conversation between himself and the King (Louis XIV) as follows :—

The King. ' It seems to me that such a man would have difficulty in getting on his horse, and being on to help himself.'

De Pluvinel. ' It would be very difficult, but with this arming the matter has been provided for. In this manner at triumphs and tourneys there ought to be at the two ends of the lists a small scaffold, the height of a stirrup, on which two or three persons can stand, that is to say, the knight, an armourer to arm him, and one other to help him. The knight being armed and the horse brought close to the stand, he easily mounts him.'

Reference has been made to the fact that modern writers call the sliding rivet the ' Almain ' rivet. Whenever mentioned in Inventories and such-like documents, the Almain rivet stands for a suit of light armour. Garrard, in his *Art of Warre* (1591), distinctly says, ' The fore part of a corselet and a head peece and tasses is the almayne rivet.' Among the purchases made on the Continent by Henry VIII in 1512 may be noted 2,000 Almain rivets, each consisting of a salet, a gorget, a breastplate, a backplate, and a pair of splints (short taces). In the Inventory of the goods of Dame Agnes Huntingdon, executed at Tyburn for murdering her husband in 1523, we find ' sex score pare of harness of Alman rivets '. The ' pare ', of course, refers to the breast- and backplates. The word Alman, Almaine, or Almain, shows that the invention of this light armour and the sliding rivets which were used in its construction came from Germany.

That the wearing of armour caused grave inconvenience to some, while to others it seems to have been no hindrance at all, we may gather from the following historical incidents. In 1526 King Louis of Hungary, fleeing from the Battle of Mohacz, was drowned while crossing the Danube because of the weight of his armour. On the other hand we find that Robert de Vere, Earl of Oxford, when forced to fly at the Battle of Radcot Bridge, escaped easily by swimming the river to safety in full armour. We should remember that the weight of plate armour was less felt than that of mail, because the former was distributed over the whole body and limbs, while the latter hung from the shoulders and waist alone. King Henry V, in courting Queen Katharine, says :—' If I could win a lady at leapfrog, or by vaulting into my saddle with my armour on my back,' which seems to imply that this feat was at any rate a possibility. Oliver de la Marche describes Galliot de Balthasin in 1446 as leaping clear out of his saddle ' Armé de toute '. We may safely consign Sir Walter Scott's description of the feasting knights to the realms of poetic licence, for he writes :—

> They carved at the meal with gloves of steel
> And drank the red wine through their helmets barred.

Now if there were two portions of the knight's equipment which would be put off at the first opportunity, and which could be assumed the most rapidly, they were the helmet and gauntlets. To drink through a visored helmet is a practical impossibility. The word Beavor, which is generally derived from the Italian *bevere*, to drink, has been considered by Baron de Cosson, with far more probability, to be derived from the Old French *bavière* (originally = a child's bib, from *bave*, saliva).

The cleaning of armour is frequently alluded to in Inventories. In the Dover Castle Inventory of 1344 is mentioned ' i barrelle pro armaturis rollandis '. Chain-mail was rolled in barrels with sand and vinegar to clean it, just as, inversely, barrels are cleaned in the country at the present day by rolling chains in them. The mending and cleaning of armour was of the first importance, and the travelling knight took with him an armourer who was provided with such things as ' oil for dressing my lord's harness, a thousand armyng nayles (rivets) a payre of pynsores, pomyshe (pumice stone), fylles, a hammer and all other stuffe and tools belonginge to an armorer '.[1]

We can gather but little of the methods of the armourers in their work. It was so important a craft that its operations were most jealously guarded, and the term ' Mystery ', which was applied to the Trade Gilds of the Middle Ages, can be most fittingly given to that of the armour-smith. In the *Weisskunig* of Hans Burgkmair, the noted German engraver, appears an interesting woodcut of the young Maximilian in the workshop of Conrad Seusenhofer, the famous armourer. In the text the master-smith is described as being anxious to make use of the ' forbidden art ', but the young king replies, ' Arm me according to my own taste, for it is I, not you, who have to take part in the tournament.' What this forbidden art may have been we have no suggestion given us. It seems, from this account, to be more than likely that Seusenhofer possessed some mechanical means for stamping out armour plate ; for it goes on to say, ' So this young King invented a new art for warriors' armour, so that in the workshop 30 front pieces and 30 hinder pieces were made at once. How wonderful and skilful was this King ! '

A most interesting album of designs by one ' Jacobe ', who has been identified by the late Herr Wendelin Boeheim as Jacobe Topf, is now, after many vicissitudes, in the Art Library of the Victoria and Albert Museum, South Kensington. From the somewhat naïve treatment of the designs they can hardly be considered to be working drawings, but were more probably sketches submitted to the different patrons of the armourer and kept for reference. The Album has been reproduced in facsimile, with a preface giving its history and verifying the suits drawn on its pages, by Viscount

[1] *Arch. Journ.*, vol. lx.

Dillon, Curator of the Tower Armouries. Space will not admit of more notice of this unique volume. Its author seems to have worked almost entirely for the nobles of the court of Queen Elizabeth ; only two of the designs were made for foreigners. Of the famous armourers of Italy, the Missaglias, Negrolis, and Campi; and of the great Colman family, Seusenhofer and Wolf, the master-craftsmen of Germany, we can do no more than mention the names.

Experts in armour, like Baron de Cosson and Herr Boeheim, have in the various archaeological journals of England and Germany brought to light many interesting facts about these armourers, but the confines of this handbook do not admit of detailed quotation, nor, indeed, is it necessary to study these details till the primary interest in defensive armour has been aroused. When this has been achieved the student will certainly leave no records unexamined in following to its farthest extremes this most fascinating study.[1]

FIG. 32. Archer wearing jack. From the Beauchamp Pageants, fifteenth century.

It is almost superfluous to discuss the third of our axioms, namely, that which concerns the confession of material. All armour of the best periods does this to the full. It is only under the blighting influence of the Renaissance that we find metal so worked that it resembles woven fabrics, or, worse still, the human form and features. The limited space at our disposal precludes us from investigating the various Coats of Fence, or body protections of quilted fabrics with metal, horn, and other materials added. Mention has been made in the chapter on the Transition of the Brigandine, which formed a very serviceable defence without being

---

[1] Boeheim, *Meister der Waffenschmiedkunst*; De Cosson, *Arch. Journ.,* vol. xlviii.

so unwieldy as the suit of plate. There are several of these brigandines in English and European armouries. These defences weigh as much as 18 lb., and are made of many small pieces of metal. An example in the Tower contains 1,164.[1]   Fig. 32, from the Beauchamp Pageants (Cotton MS., Julius E. iv), shows an archer of the year 1485 wearing the jack over a shirt of mail. The Jack was used by the rank and file, and was stuffed and wadded or composed of plates of metal or horn laced together with string between layers of leather or linen.

[1] *Arch. Journ.*, lx.

CHAPTER IV

PLATE ARMOUR (1410–about 1600)

It is so very rare to be able to fix the date of a suit of armour at a particular year that we are forced, in dividing our periods of defensive armour with any degree of minuteness, to have recourse to the records existing in monumental effigies. The earliest brasses which show the whole suit of plate without camail or jupon are those of one of the d'Eresby family at Spilsby, Lincolnshire, and of Sir John Wylcotes at Great Tew, Oxon., both dated 1410. In these brasses we find that the camail has become the Standard of Mail, or collarette, worn under the gorget of plate. The hauberk is seen beneath the taces and, in the former brass, in the '*défaut de la cuirasse*', or unprotected part at the junction of arm and body. In the Great Tew brass this part is protected by oval plates which, as we have noticed in a preceding chapter, are called motons or besagues. Hewitt does not seem to have come across these terms in the course of his very minute investigations, but calls them Croissants or Gouchets. He quotes a passage from Mathieu de Coucy's *History of Charles VII* (p. 560) which runs :—' au-dessous du bras at au vif de son harnois, par faute et manque d'y avoir un croissant ou gouchet.' Haines, in his *Monumental Brasses*, mentions the moton, but assigns this name to a piece of plate rarely met with, shaped to fit under the right armpit only. With the disappearance of the jupon we see the body defence exposed to view. The breast-plate is globular in form, and below the waist we see the taces or laminated strips of plate overlapping each other, which at this early period were attached to a leather lining. As we have seen in the chapter on the Construction of Armour, at a later period these taces were held together by sliding rivets, which allowed a certain amount of vertical play. Plate armour, during the earlier years of the fifteenth century, was naturally in a somewhat experimental state, and we find frequent examples of the old forms and fashions in contemporary representations. About the year 1440 appears a distinct style, called 'Gothic', which, of all types of defensive armour, is perhaps the most graceful. This term, 'Gothic,' is as inappropriate, in the relation which it bore, to armour as to architecture; but its use is so general that we must perforce adopt it for want of a better. The salient points of Gothic armour are the sweeping lines embossed on its surfaces (Plate VIII). The cuirass is generally made in two pieces, an upper and a lower, which allows more freedom for the body. From the taces are hung Tassets, ending in a point towards the lower edge. The later form of Gothic breastplate is longer, and the taces fewer in number. Armour was so frequently remade to suit later fashions, or, from lack of antiquarian interest, so often destroyed, that there is little of this Gothic armour existing in England, except those suits which have been acquired from the Continent by private collectors or public museums. Almost all of them are incomplete, or, if complete, have been restored—particularly the leg armour—at a recent date. Perhaps the finest example of this style is to be found on the 'Beauchamp' effigy in St. Mary's Church, Warwick. Space will not allow of a full account of the documents connected with the making of this magnificent figure, which was executed by Will. Austin, a bronze-founder, and Bartholomew Lambespring, a goldsmith, in 1454, fifteen years after the death of the Earl. All these interesting details are given very fully in Blore's *Monumental Remains*. To students of the constructional side of armour this monument is particularly valuable because all the fastenings, rivets, and straps are conscientiously portrayed, not only on the front, but also at the back. Charles Stothard, the antiquary, when making drawings of the figure for his work on *Monumental Effigies*, turned it over and discovered this example of the care and technical ability of the makers. The breastplate is short, and consequently the taces are more numerous than when the breastplate is longer. They consist of five lames. From the taces hang four tassets, two bluntly pointed in front, and two much shorter, and more sharply pointed, over the hip-bones. The taces are hinged at the side for convenience in putting on and off. The coudes are large and of the butterfly-wing type, and the sollerets are of normal length. In many of the Gothic suits these sollerets, following the custom in civil dress, were extravagantly long and pointed. This form is called ' à la poulaine ', while the shorter kind are known as ' demi-poulaine '.

Some writers are apt to confuse this term ' poulaine ' with ' poleyne ', the knee-cop used in the earlier days of the Transition Period ; it is needless to point out that they are quite distinct. Baron de Cosson has put forward a most interesting theory in connexion with this effigy. He finds a close resemblance between the armour here portrayed and that shown in the picture of St. George, by Mantegna, in the Accademia at Venice. The Earl of Warwick, who is represented on this monument, is known to have been at Milan in his youth, and to have taken part in tournaments at Verona ; so it is more than probable that he ordered his armour from the Milanese armourers, of whom the famous Missaglia family were the chief craftsmen, and who made some fine suits of this Gothic style.

The next distinctive style to be noticed is called the ' Maximilian '. It can hardly be said that this new design was evolved from the Gothic, though of necessity there must be a certain similarity between them, at least in constructional detail. It is more likely, when we consider the individuality of the young Maximilian, especially as recorded in Hans Burgkmair's *Weisskunig*, and his interest in every art, craft, and trade, that it was a fashion made, so to speak, to order. The Maximilian Period of armour may be said to last from about 1500 to 1540. It is distinguished by the radiating fluted channels that spread from a central point in the breastpiece, closely resembling the

PLATE VIII

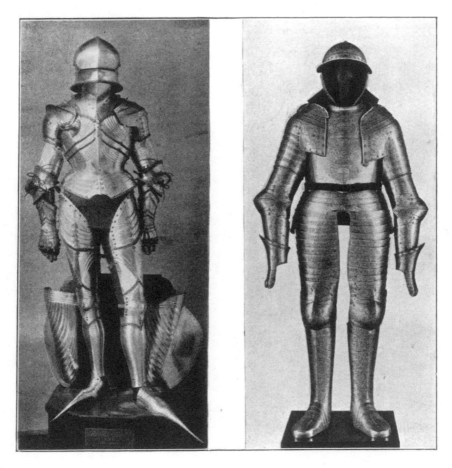

ARMOUR OF
(1) Archduke Sigismond of Tyrol, 1470,   (2) Louis XIV of France, 1680.

flutings of the scallop-shell (Fig. 24). The main lines of the
suit are heavier and more clumsy than those of the Gothic
variety. The breastplate is shorter, globose in form, and made
in one piece as distinct from the Gothic breastplate, which was
generally composed of an upper and lower portion. The pauldrons
are larger and the upstanding neck-guards more pronounced. The

FIG. 33. Gothic suit. Turin
Armoury.

FIG. 34. Maximilian suit. Vienna
Armoury, 1523.

coude and genouillière are both smaller than in the Gothic suit,
and fit more closely to the limbs. In imitation of the civilian dress
the solleret becomes shorter and broader in the toe. This variety
is known as the 'bec de cane' or 'bear-paw' solleret. Some
writers use the term Sabaton for the foot-defence of this period.
This term is found (sabataynes) in the Hastings manuscript referred
to in the preceding chapter. The pauldrons of the Maximilian

suit are generally of unequal size ; that for the right arm being
smaller, to admit of the couching of the lance under the armpit
(Fig. 34). The tassets are made in two or more pieces, connected
with the strap and sliding rivet described in the preceding chapter.
The fluting on the Maximilian armour is not without practical purpose, for, besides presenting the 'glancing' surface, which has been
before referred to, it gives increased strength and rigidity without
much extra weight. A modern example of this is to be found in the
corrugated iron used for roofing, which will stand far greater
pressure than will the same thickness of metal used flat.

It is at this period of the history of defensive armour that we
first find traces of that decadence which later on permeated every
art and craft with its pernicious poison. It is to be found in the
imitating of fabrics and also of the human face in metal. There
exist suits of plate in many museums, both in England and on the
Continent, in which the puffings and slashings of the civilian attire
are closely copied in embossed metal, entirely destroying the
important glancing surfaces on which we have laid such stress. It
is alleged that this fashion in civilian dress was intended to suggest,
by the cutting of the material to show an undergarment beneath,
that the wearer was a fighting man who had seen rough service.
If this be the case it is the more reprehensible that metal should
be treated in a similar manner ; for hard usage would dent, but
it would not tear. A portion of one of these debased suits is drawn
on Fig. 42.

It must not be supposed that all armour at this period was
fluted. There was still a good deal which had a plain surface,
and this plain armour continued to be used after the Maximilian
armour had been given up. It may have been that the evil
genius of the Renaissance pointed to the plain surfaces as ex-
cellent fields for the skill of the decorator, a field which the
strongly-marked flutings of the Maximilian armour could not
offer. At first this decoration was confined to engraved borders,
or, if the design covered the whole suit, it was so lightly engraved
that the smooth surface was in no way impaired, though perhaps

some of the dignified simplicity of the plain metal was lost. An instance of this proper application of ornament to armour is to be found in the ' Seusenhofer ' suit in the Tower (Plate VI), made to the order of the Emperor Maximilian for Henry VIII. It is one of the finest suits of this period in existence. The ornament is lightly engraved all over it, and includes representations of the legends of St. George and St. Barbara. Instead of taces and tassets the lower part of the body and the thighs are protected by steel Bases made in folds to imitate the skirts worn in civilian dress. It will be remembered that in the preceding chapter a conversation between Seusenhofer and the young Maximilian was quoted, and when we study this suit carefully we feel that the young king did wisely in the choice of his master-armourer. The craftsman's Poinçon or mark is to be found at the back of the helmet.

If space but permitted we might devote many pages to the work of the great armour-smiths as exemplified in the armouries of Madrid and Vienna. It is difficult, at this period of history, to generalize at all satisfactorily. Each suit is, in many ways, distinct from its neighbour, just as the character and personality of the wearers differed. The young Maximilian's words to Seusenhofer, ' Arm me according to my own taste,' is true of every suit that we examine, for it is evident that each man had his own favourite fashion or, from physical necessity, was provided with some special variation from the usual form. An instance of this may be noted in the Barendyne helm at Haseley Church, near Thame, in which an extra plate has been added at the lower edge of the helm to suit the length of neck of the last wearer.

As the experience of the armourer increased, and as the science of war developed, the armed man trusted more to the fixed defences of his person than to the more primitive protection of the movable shield. In the tilt-yard and also in war the mounted man endeavoured to present his left side to his adversary. On consideration the reason for this will be plain, for the right arm was required to be free and, as far as possible, unhampered by heavy armour, but the left arm, held at rest at the bridle, could be covered with as heavy defences as the wearer might choose. This form of unequal arming is well shown on the Frontispiece. The left shoulder wears a large pauldron with a high neck-guard, and the elbow wears the passe-guard which we have noticed in detail in the preceding chapter. The leg armour in this suit should be noticed, for it is extremely fine and graceful in line, and yet proclaims its material. The suit of Henry VIII (Plate VI) is a good specimen of armour of the Maximilian period, but without the flutings which generally distinguish this style of plate. The neck-guards are high and the large coudes show the glancing surface plainly. This detail also is shown on the fan plates at the genouillières, which in the Tower Inventories are called by the more English term ' knee-cops '. The bridle-hand of the rider wears the Manifer (main-de-fer). Those writers who still follow blindly the incorrect nomenclature of Meyrick give the name Mainfaire or Manefer to the Crinet or neck defence of the horse. How this absurd play upon words can ever have been taken seriously passes understanding.

The manifer is solely the rigid iron gauntlet for the bridle-hand, where no sudden or complicated movement of the wrist or fingers was needed ; another instance of the difference in arming the two sides of the body. This difference of arming is more noticeable in the jousting armour, for in military sports, especially during the sixteenth century, the object of the contestants was to score points rather than to injure each other. We find, therefore, such pieces as the Grand-guard, and with it the Volant piece, the Passe-guard, the Poldermitton—so called from its likeness to the ' épaule de mouton ', and worn over the bend of the right arm—and the various reinforcing breastplates which were screwed on to the left side of the tilting suit to offer a more rigid defence and also to present additional glancing surface to the lance-point. In some varieties of joust a small wooden shield was fastened to the left breast, and when this was the case the heavy pauldron was dispensed with. The large Vamplate (Plate XI) sufficiently protected the right arm from injury. The Nuremberg suit (Plate VII) shows

this form of arming for the joust. The great helm is firmly screwed
to the back and breast, the two holes on the left side of the breastplate are for the attachment of the shield, the rigid bridle-cuff
covers the left hand, and the curved elbow-guard—this is not the
passe-guard—protects the bend of the left arm as the poldermitton
protects the right. The large circular disc defends the *vif de l'harnois*, and is *bouché* or notched at its lower end to allow the lance
to be couched, resting on the curved lance-rest in front and lodged
under the Queue at the back. The legs, in this variety of joust,
were not armed ; for the object of the jousters was to unhorse
each other, and it was necessary to have perfect freedom in gripping
the horse's sides. Sometimes a great plate of metal, curved to
cover the leg, was worn to protect the wearer from the shock of
impact. This was called the Dilge, or Tilting Cuisse, which is shown
on Plate VIII behind the figure of Count Sigismond, and also on
Plate VII. The large-bowed saddle also was used for this end.
There is one of these saddles in the Tower which measures nearly
5 feet in height. Behind the saddle-bow are two rings which
encircled the rider's legs. It is needless to point out that in this
form of joust the object was to break lances and not to unhorse ;
for, if the latter were intended, the rider stood a good chance of
breaking his legs owing to his rigid position in the saddle.

The Tonlet suit (Fig. 35) was used solely for fighting on foot.
The bell-shaped skirt of plate was so constructed with the sliding
rivets or straps which have been before referred to, that it could
be pulled up and down. Sometimes the lower lame could be taken
off altogether. When fighting with axes or swords in the lists this
plate skirt presented a glancing surface to the weapon and protected the legs. The tonlet is variously called by writers upon
armour, Bases, Lamboys, or Jamboys ; of the two latter terms
jamboys is the more correct. The Bases were originally the cloth
skirts in vogue in civilian dress at the time of Henry VIII, and
when defensive armour followed civilian fashion the name came
to be applied to the steel imitation.

Towards the end of the sixteenth century we find the weight

of the war harness gradually decrease. The richly-ornamented
suits which mark this period were in no way suited for any practical
purpose and were used only for parades. Extended campaigns
and long marches necessitated lighter equipment, and we find in
contemporary records instances, not only of the men-at-arms discarding their armour owing to its inconvenience, but also of

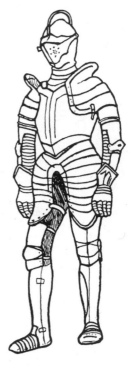

FIG. 35. Tonlet suit.
Madrid.

FIG. 36. War suit, 1547.
Vienna Armoury.

commanders ordering them to lighten their equipment for greater
rapidity of movement. Sir Richard Hawkins, in his *Observations*
on his voyage into the South Sea (1593), writes: 'I had great
preparation of armours as well of proofe as of light corsletts, yet
not a man would use them, but esteemed a pott of wine a better
defence than an armour of proofe.' Again, Sir John Smythe, in
his *Instructions, Observations and Orders Militarie* (1595), writes:
. . . ' I saw but very few of that army (at the camp at Tilbury)

PLATE IX

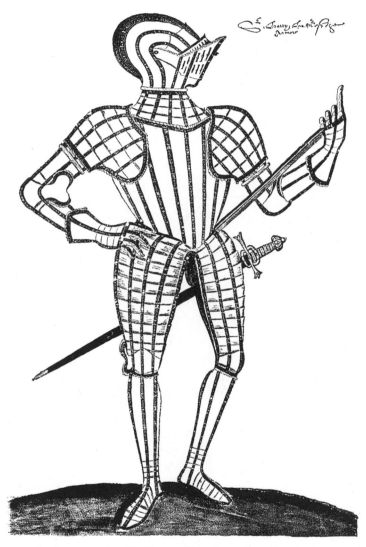

Design for a suit of armour for Sir Henry Lee, from the *Almain Armourer's Album*.

that had any convenience of apparrell to arme withal.' Edward Davies, in 1619, mentions the fact that men armed ' with a heavie shirt of mail and a burganet, by that time they have marched in the heat of summer or deepe of winter ten or twelve English miles, they are apt more to rest than readie to fight '. As early as the year 1364 we find that at the Battle of Auray Sir Hugh Calverley ordered his men to take off their cuisses that they might move more rapidly. In the armour of the late sixteenth century one of the chief points of difference from the former fashions is to be found in the cuisses. Whereas these defences were formerly made of one, or possibly two plates, we now find them laminated from waist to knee and joined by the strap and sliding rivet arrangement which we have noted in the arm defences and tassets. The tassets are now no longer used (Fig. 36). Very soon the jambs were given up in favour of buff boots, and when once this was established the next step was the half suit which will be noticed in a succeeding chapter.

After the fourteenth century the great helm was but seldom used for war, but for jousting it was still retained, and, as this form of military sport was practised more scientifically, so the weight and shape of the helm were made to suit the necessary conditions. The Brocas helm (Plate V) is the finest example of English helm of this period ; it weighs 22 lb. The other known examples of home manufacture are the Westminster helm, which was discovered in the Triforium of Westminster Abbey in 1869, and weighs 17 lb. 12 oz.; the Dawtray helm at Petworth (21 lb. 8 oz.) ; the Barendyne helm at Haseley, near Thame ($13\frac{1}{2}$ lb.) ; the Fogge helm at Ashford, Sussex (24 lb.); the Wallace helm, in the collection at Hertford House (17 lb.) ; and the great headpiece in the possession of Captain Lindsay of Sutton Courtenay, Abingdon, which turns the scale at 25 lb. 14 oz. It will be seen from the weight of these helms that they could only be used for the jousting course and were put off on the first opportunity. The details of their construction have been noticed in Chapter III.

On referring to Plate V it will be seen that the bascinet was the precursor of the Salade, which may be considered the typical headpiece of the fifteenth century. The rear peak of the bascinet is prolonged over the neck, and in a later form of German origin the peak is hinged to allow the wearer to throw back his head with ease. The ocularium, or vision slit, is sometimes cut in the front of the salade, but more often it is found in a pivoted visor which could be thrown back. The Beavor is generally a separate piece strapped round the neck or, in tilting, bolted to the breastplate. Some writers call this the Mentonière, but this name should rather be applied to the tilting breastplate which also protected the lower portion of the face. Shakespeare uses the term beavor very loosely, and frequently means by it the whole helmet.

The German 'Schallern', or salade, so called from its shell-like form, seems to have been evolved from the chapel-de-fer or war-hat by contracting the brim at the sides and prolonging it at the back. In fact, in Chastelain's account of the fight between Jacques de Lalain and Gérard de Roussillon the salade worn by Messire Jacques is described as ' un chapeau de fer d'ancienne façon '.[1] The salade was often richly decorated. Baron de Cosson, in the preface to the Catalogue of Helmets exhibited at the Archaeological Institute in June, 1880[2], instances a salade made for the Duke of Burgundy in 1443, which was valued at 10,000 crowns of gold. More modest decoration was obtained by covering the salade with velvet and fixing ornaments over this of gilded iron or brass. There are several of these covered salades in the various collections in England and on the Continent. Sometimes the salade was painted, as we see in an example in the Tower.

The Armet, or close helmet, followed the salade, and is mentioned by Oliver de la Marche as early as 1443.[3] The name is supposed to be a corruption of ' heaumet ', the diminutive of ' heaume', the great helm of the fourteenth century.[4] Whereas the salade is in form a hat-like defence, the armet fits the head closely

[1] G. Chastelain, p. 679.　　　　　　　　　[2] *Arch. Journ.*, xxxvii.
[3] Oliver de la Marche, p. 288.
[4] N.E. Dict. gives Armette, a diminutive of Arme. Armez is also found.

and can only be put on by opening the helmet, as is shown on Plate V and Fig. 31. The various parts of the armet have been already described in Chapter III. The armet does not appear in monumental effigies in England before the reign of Henry VIII. The English were never in a hurry to take up new fashions in armour; being to a large extent dependent on the work of foreign craftsmen, they seem to have waited to prove the utility of an innovation before adopting it. Against this, however, we must place the fact that in the picture at Hampton Court of the meeting of Henry VIII and Maximilian, the English are all shown wearing armets, while the Germans still wear the salade. The armet on the Seusenhofer suit in the Tower, which has been noticed in this chapter, is a very perfect example of this style of headpiece.

The Burgonet is an open helmet, and, as the name implies, of Burgundian origin. To those students who consult Meyrick it is advisable to give a word of warning as to this author's theory of the burgonet. He assumes that it is a variety of the armet, but with a grooved collar which fitted over the gorget. His authority for this assertion is a single reference in the *Origines des Chevaliers Armoriés et Heraux*, by Fauchet.[1] Space will not allow of the investigation of this authority, but Baron de Cosson in the Catalogue above quoted effectively disposes of Meyrick's theory.[2] The salient points of the burgonet, as may be seen on Plate V, are the Umbril or brim projecting over the eyes, and the upstanding comb or (in some cases) three combs that appear on the skull-piece. In the best examples these combs are forged with the skull out of one piece of metal, a *tour de force* in craftsmanship that could hardly be surpassed. The ear-flaps are hinged at the sides, and at the base of the skull is fixed the Panache, or plume-holder. The face-guard, when used with the burgonet, is called the Buffe,[3] and, like the beavor worn with the salade, is held in place by a strap round the neck. This form of helmet was chiefly used by light cavalry.

[1] Paris, 1606, fol. 42. See Cat. of Helmets, *Arch. Journ.*, xxxvii.

[2] *Arch. Journ.*, xxxvii.

[3] The term *Bufe* is sometimes wrongly used for the upright shoulder-guards on the pauldron.

The Morion and the Cabasset are both helmets worn by foot-soldiers, and appear about the middle of the sixteenth century. The cabasset is generally to be distinguished by the curious little point projecting from the apex. Often the comb and upturned brim of the morion are extravagant in form and tend to make the helmet exceedingly heavy and inconvenient.

The shields of the fifteenth and sixteenth century were more for display than for use, except in the tilt-yard. As we have seen, the development of plate armour, especially on the left side, made the shield not only unnecessary, but also inconvenient. In the joust, however, where it was important that the lance should find no hold on a vital part of the body, such as the juncture of the arm, the shield was used to glance the weapon off, or, where unhorsing was the object, it was ribbed with diagonally crossing ridges to give the lance-point a surer hold. The Pavis or Pavoise (Fig. 37) was more generally used by archers and crossbowmen as a cover. A good specimen of the pavis exists in the Ashmolean Museum at Oxford, and there are two large examples of heavier make with peepholes for the archer, and wooden props as shown in our illustration, at Brussels and Berlin.

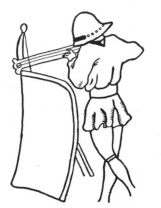

FIG. 37. Pavis. Cotton MS. Julius E. iv, 1485.

PLATE X

Horse armour of the Emperor Maximilian. Tower.

CHAPTER V

HORSE ARMOUR

THE fully-equipped knight, whether in the cumbrous garments of mail or in the more adaptable suit of plate, was so entirely dependent on his horse, both in active warfare and in the tilt-yard, that some notice of the defences of the Destrier or war-horse is necessary in this short examination of the history of defensive armour. On the Bayeux Tapestry there is no suggestion of armour of any kind upon the horses, but Wace writes in the *Roman de Rou* (line 12,627)—

> Vint Williame li filz Osber
> Son cheval tot covert de fer.

We should remember, however, that Wace wrote in the second half of the twelfth century and, like the other chroniclers of the Middle Ages, both in picture and text, portrayed his characters in the dress of his own time. The Trapper of mail shown on Fig. 38 is taken from Stothard's drawing of one of the paintings in the Painted Chamber at Westminster, now destroyed.[1] These decorations are supposed to have been executed about the year 1237. Here the horse is shown covered with a most inconvenient housing of mail, which can hardly have been in very general use, in this particular form at any rate ; for it would be almost impossible for a horse to walk, let alone to trot or gallop, with such a defence. The textile trapper was, of course, lighter, and was used merely for ornament and display, though it may have been designed, as the surcoat was, to protect the mail defence beneath from wet.

Jean Chartier, in his *Histoire de Charles VI* (p. 257), states that sometimes these rich trappings or housings were, after the death of their owner, bequeathed to churches, where they were used for

[1] *Monumenta Vetusta*, vol. vi.

altar hangings, or inversely, when trappings were needed, the churches were despoiled of their embroideries to provide them.

The mailed horse appears as early as the Roman period, and is shown on the Column of Trajan, but in Europe he does not seem to have been commonly in use much before the thirteenth century. As the man was sometimes defended entirely by garments of quilted fabrics, so the horse also wore pourpointed housings. We can only surmise, from the folds and lines shown on seals or drawings, which variety is intended ; but the stiff lines of the housing

Fig. 38. Trapper of Mail, from the Painted Chamber, Westminster, thirteenth century.

Fig. 39. Ivory chessman, from Hewitt's *Ancient Armour*, fourteenth century.

on the seal of Roger de Quinci, Earl of Winchester (1219–64), and its raised lozenges, seem to suggest a thicker substance than does the more flowing drapery on Fig. 11. Matthew Paris, in describing the Battle of Nuova Croce in 1237, writes that ' A credible Italian asserted that Milan with its dependencies raised an army of six thousand men-at-arms with iron-clad horses '. An ordinance of Philip the Fair, in 1303, provides that every holder of an estate of 500 livres rental should furnish a man at-arms well mounted on a horse ' couvert de couvertures de fer ou de couverture pourpointe'. The caparisoned horse first appears on royal seals in the reign of Edward I. In the Roll of Purchases of Windsor Park Tournament (1278), the horses are provided with parchment crests, and the Clavoncs or rivets used for fixing these crests are mentioned in the Wardrobe Accounts of Edward I in 1300: ' cum clavis argenti pro eodem capello.' The earliest note we have of a rigid defence for the horse is in the Windsor Roll, which contains the following item :—' D Milon le Cuireur xxxviij

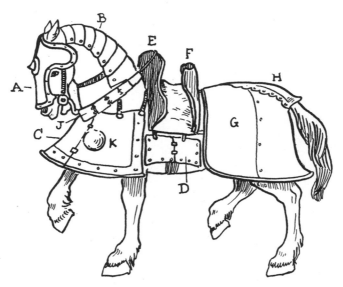

FIG. 40.   Horse armour.   A, Chamfron ; B, Crinet ; C, Peytral ; D, Flanchards ; E, Arçon ; F, Cantel ; G, Crupper ; H, Tail-guard ; J, Metal rein-guard ; K, Glancing-knob.

copita cor de similitud' capit equoz.' This headpiece was of leather, either used in its natural state or as cuirbouilli, and seems to be the material suggested in the ivory chessman (Fig. 39) illustrated in Hewitt (vol. ii, p. 314). In the Will of the Earl of Surrey (1347) is mentioned a breastpiece of leather for a horse. In the fifteenth century we find the horse protected with plate like his rider, and usually the lines of the Barding or horse armour follow those of the man. Fig. 40 shows the armed horse with the various portions of his defence named.

The Chamfron is sometimes provided with hinged cheek-plates

and usually has a holder for a plume. On the forehead are often shown the arms of the owner or a tapered spike. Angellucci, in his preface to the Catalogue of the Turin Armoury, differentiates between the chamfron (tesera) and the Frontale or plate protecting the front of the head alone. There are fine suits of Gothic horse armour both in the Musée d'Artillerie in Paris and also in the Wallace Collection at Hertford House. The latter is one of the best-arranged mounted suits in existence. The different pieces of the horse armour bear the delicate sweeping lines embossed on the surface in the same way that the armour of the man is treated. The restored linings of leather and skin show how the horse was protected from the chafing of the metal. The Peytral or Poitrel is hung from the neck and withers, and is frequently provided with large bosses, called *Bossoirs, Pezoneras,* or *Glancing-knobs,* to direct the lance-thrust away from the horse. It is often hinged in three pieces. The Flanchards hang from the saddle on either side, and are sometimes, as on Plate IV and the Frontispiece, curved upwards in the centre to admit of the use of the spur. The back of the horse is protected by the Croupière or Crupper, which is made up of several pieces riveted or hinged together. The root of the tail is covered by a tubular plate called the Gardequeue, which is often moulded into the form of a dragon or dolphin. All these plates were lined with leather or wadded with cotton to prevent chafing. Often, however, cuirbouilli was used instead of metal and was richly decorated with painting and gilding. A picture of the Battle of Pavia in the Ashmolean Museum, Oxford, shows many of these painted bards, and the same material is doubtless intended in the relief of the Battle of Brescia on the Visconti monument at Pavia. These leather bards have entirely disappeared and are not to be found in any collections except for a portion of a crupper of this material in the Tower. The saddle, with its high Arciones or peaks, back and front, was in itself an efficacious protection for the waist and loins. The term Cantle is sometimes used for either plate, but it is generally accepted as the name for the rear peak. Both this part and the front plate are often covered with metal.

The great jousting saddles have been noticed in the preceding chapter. The reins are protected from being cut by hinged plates, as shown on Plate X.[1]

These pieces constitute the armour of the horse as usually found in museums and in painting and sculpture. There is, however, in the Zeughaus in Vienna a curious portrait of Harnisch-meister Albrecht, dated 1480. The horse on which he rides is armed completely with plate except for an aperture in the flanchards for using the spur. The legs are covered with hinged and bolted defences very similar to those of the armour for men. It might be supposed that this was but a fantastic idea of the painter, if Viscount Dillon had not discovered a Cuissard, or thigh-piece, which much resembles those shown on the picture, in the Musée de la Porte de Hal, Brussels. In the days of the Decadence, when the craft of the armourer was to a great extent overwhelmed by the riotous fancy of the decorator, the horse shared with his rider in this display. The armour shown on Plate X, known as the Burgundian armour from the badges of the Emperor Maximilian which adorn it, does not offend in this respect, because the embossing serves to give rigidity to the metal without interfering with its defensive qualities. The same may be said of the barding shown on the Frontispiece, but on Plate IV the loss of dignity in line, and the embossed hemisphere—which, for its purpose, should be smooth—show the beginning of the decay in constructional skill. The highly ornamented pageant armour made for the Elector Christian II, now in the Dresden Museum, though extraordinarily perfect in workmanship, should be classed rather as the work of goldsmith or sculptor than as that of the armourer.

---

[1] This is *not* the ' garde-rein '.   See p. 62.

CHAPTER VI

THE DECADENCE OF ARMOUR

IN the practice of any of the crafts, or applied arts as they are now called, the surest and most manifest signs of decadence are to be found in two aspects of that craft. The first of these is that which refers to the material used. With regard to armour this

FIG. 41. Grotesque helmet, sixteenth century. Nuremberg.

consideration is faithfully adhered to in most examples of the armourer's work up to the end of the fifteenth century ; but by the beginning of the sixteenth century we find the craftsman becoming wearied of his technical perfection and the simplicity and constructional dignity which invariably accompanies such perfection. His efforts are now directed to fashioning his metal into such forms as in no way suggest his material, but only show a certain meretricious skill in workmanship. Fig. 41 shows a very favourite form of this artistic incoherence. The defensive properties of the helmet are in no way increased, but rather are annulled by presenting hollows and projections where before a smooth surface existed. It is superfluous to point out the grotesque and bizarre effect of this human face in metal.[1] Another instance of this wilful disregard of material is to be noticed in those suits which imitate the puffed and slashed dress in fashion for civilian wear during the sixteenth century. Many of these suits exist in English and European armouries, which proves that they were popular,

[1] That this fashion in helmets was a general one we may judge from the fact that most armouries possess examples of these human-faced helmets.

but to the true craftsman there is something degrading in the efforts of the expert ironworker, expending his energies, not to produce a finely constructed piece of work, but rather to imitate the seams and pipings of the work of a tailor or dressmaker ; and, however much we may admire his technical skill, we must, perforce, place his artistic aspirations side by side with the ' grainer and marbler ' who was so conspicuous a factor in domestic decoration in the middle of the nineteenth century. Fig. 42 shows this decadence carried to its furthest pitch. By the middle of the sixteenth century the Renaissance, which had been, in the first instance, the birth of all that is best in European art and craftsmanship, became a baneful influence. The expert painter, having mastered the intricacies of his art, turned them into extravagant channels and exaggerated action; foreshortened figures and optical illusions took the place of the dignified compositions of the earlier period. Nor could the crafts escape this deadly poison. To the credit of the craftsmen we may hope that the luxurious indulgence

Fig. 42. Puffed suit, sixteenth century. Vienna.[1]

and ostentatious display of the princely patron was the cause of decadence in the crafts, rather than the inclination of the workers themselves. Still the fact remains that, as soon as the plain and constructionally sound work began to be overspread with ornament, architecture, metal-work, wood-carving, and all the allied arts began to be debased from their former high position. With the decoration of armour its practical utility began to decline. It must be admitted, however, that one reason for the decoration

[1] This suit is shown with the brayette attached ; which for obvious reasons is exhibited in most armouries separate from the suit.

was that armour was, by degrees, less and less used for war and only retained for pageant, joust, and parade in which personal display and magnificence were demanded.

The engraved and inlaid suits of the late sixteenth and seventeenth centuries, although they offend the craftsman's eye as does the decorated bicycle of the Oriental potentate to-day, do not transgress that important law, on which so much stress has been laid, of offering a glancing surface to the opposing weapon. It is when we come to the embossed suits with their hollows and projections that we find the true character of armour lost and the metal used only as a material for exhibiting the dexterity of the workman without any consideration for its use or construction. This interference with the glancing surface is noticeable in the suit illustrated in Fig. 42, but even here there is some excuse, in

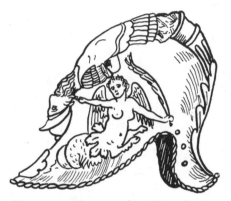

FIG. 43.   Casque after Negroli, sixteenth century.   Paris.

that the designer had reason for his embossing of the metal—if the imitation of the puffed suit was to be carefully portrayed. The same, however, cannot be urged for those suits which are simply covered with ornament with no purpose, little meaning, and less composition or design. If we set aside our opinions as to the suitability of the ornament, we are compelled to admire the wonderful technical skill which produced such pieces as the suit made for King Sebastian of Portugal by Anton Pfeffenhauser of Augsburg, and now in the Madrid Armoury. Here every deity of Olympus, the allegorical figures of Justice, Strength, and the Cardinal Virtues, crowd together with Navigation, Peace, and Victory ; Roman warriors fighting with elephants are found among Amorini, Satyrs, and Tritons ; while every inch of the metal not devoted to this encyclopaedia of history and legend is crowded with foliage and scroll-work of that debased and unnatural form which has become the branding mark of this period of the Renaissance.

It will be sufficient to give one example of this prostitution of art and craftsmanship. This helmet after Negroli (Fig. 43), and a similar example, signed by Negroli, at Madrid, show how the canons of the armourer's craft were ignored at this period. It

FIG. 44.   Pageant shield, sixteenth century.   Vienna.

is true that the casque still provides a metal covering for the head, and that the comb gives an additional protection to the skull, but when we examine the embossed figures at the side—and marvellously good the embossing is—we find lodgements for the sword or spear which would most certainly help to detach the helmet from its wearer. As to the comb, it may fairly be cited as an example of all that is artistically worst in the late Renaissance. Its technical merits only emphasize this. The warrior is laid on his back to suit the required shape of the helmet, and to give point to his position his hair is held by two figures whose attributes seem to suggest that intercrossing of birds, beasts, and fishes which delighted the decadent mind of the period. The figures are human to the waist and end in a dolphin's tail. Angels' wings spring from their shoulders and leopards' claws from the junction of tail and waist. Not content with this outrage to the dignity of art, the craftsman ends his warrior in an architectural base which has not even the slight merit of probability which the tail of the merman might offer. In short it is an example of technical skill at its highest, and artistic perception at its lowest point. The shield from the Vienna collection (Fig. 44) is another example, like King Sebastian's suit, of meaningless decoration. The strapwork does not in any way follow the lines of the shield, and the female figures seem to be introduced only to show that the craftsman could portray the human form in steel as easily as he could the more conventional ornament.

As the armourer, weary of constructional skill, turned to ornament as a means of showing to what further extent his powers could expand, so, with this change in his point of view, his constructional skill itself declined. The headpiece, which in the golden age of the armourer was forged in as few pieces as possible, is in the late seventeenth century made of many pieces, as the art of skilful forging declines. The ingenious articulations of the soleret are changed, and the foot is cased in plates which, overlapping only in one direction, preclude the easy movement of the wearer. The fine lines of leg and arm defences, which in the fifteenth and sixteenth century follow the shape of the limbs, give place to straight tubular plates which can only be likened to the modern stove-pipe. The grace and symmetry of the Gothic suit shown on Plate VIII, especially the leg armour, exemplify this merit of the best period of armour, while the suit made for Louis XIV, and the gilt suit of Charles I in the Tower, offend in the opposite direction. Another sure indication of the decadence of the craftsman is to be found in the imitation of constructional detail with no practical purpose. Examples of this may be seen in late seventeenth-century armour, where a single plate is embossed to represent several overlapping plates or lames, and also in the plentiful use of '*clous perdus*' or false rivets which are scattered broadcast on some suits in places where no rivets are needed.

To turn from the degradation of the simplicity and constructional perfection of armour to the reasons which led to its gradual disuse, we find that, after the Gothic period, armour became heavier, partly because of the shock tactics in vogue on active service and partly because, in the case of jousting armour, strength and great weight were needed to protect the wearer from vital injury, and partly because the improvement of firearms necessitated extra defence. The temper of the metal used was such that it would resist a pistol shot, as we have noticed in Chapter III; and on examining the surface of the metal we find, as in the Pembridge helm, that it is of so fine a texture that a modern knife will not leave a scratch when testing it. Therefore we must regard the weight of armour as one of the chief reasons for its disuse. Again, military tactics necessitated forced marches and longer expeditions than before; or at any rate it was discovered that when engaging in long expeditions the troops were chafed and hindered by their armour. It is somewhat curious to note that as the leg was the first part of the body to be armed with plate, so the leg armour was the first to be discarded. The jambs were the first pieces to go, and were replaced, in the case of the mounted man, by thick buff leather boots. The tassets were prolonged to the knee or—to describe this portion of the armour in a different way—the cuisses themselves were formed of riveted lames and the tassets discarded.

The helmet at the latter end of the seventeenth century is generally open and of the burgonet type. The breastplate is usually short and projects downwards at the lower portion after the fashion of the 'peascod' doublet of civilian wear. As early as 1586, at the siege of Zutphen, we find officers discarding their armour and keeping only the cuirass. From the Hatfield MSS.

we learn that a penny a day was allowed to each soldier in 1590, over and above his pay, for the wearing and carriage of his armour, because it had become the custom for the troops to give their accoutrements to the baggage-carriers when on the march : ' a matter both unseemly for soldiers and also very hurtful unto the armour by bruising and breaking thereof, whereby it becometh unserviceable.' In Cruso's *Militarie Instructions for the Cavallrie* (1632), we find that the arquebusiers had wholly left off their armour in favour of buff coats. Turner's *Pallas Armata* (1670)

FIG. 45. Cromwellian pikeman. Tower.

mentions the armour of officers as ' a headpiece, a corslet and a gorget, the captain having a plume of feathers in his helmet, the lieutenant not '. Further on we read, ' now the feathers you may peradventure find, but the headpiece for the most part is laid aside.' Fig. 45 shows that half armour was still worn during the Commonwealth, but by the Restoration very little was retained except for ceremonial use. As far as can be gleaned from contemporary letters and histories, Charles I never wore either the somewhat cumbrous gilt suit which is shown at the Tower or the more graceful half suit of blued steel in which Vandyke represented him in his equestrian portrait. All the metal defence we can be sure he actually wore is a steel broad-brimmed hat covered with velvet. The headpiece used by the cavalry during the Civil War is of the same type as No. 11 on Plate IV, a variety of the burgonet with a movable nasal. The breastplate continued to be worn during the wars of Marlborough, but that, too, was discarded when the efficacy of the musket proved its uselessness. The last survival of plate armour is to be found in the gorget. This became smaller as the uniform was changed, and in the end was simply a small crescent of brass hung at the neck. It was worn by infantry officers up to the year 1830, at which date it was given up in England.

The last official use of full plate armour was at the Coronation of George IV, when the King's Champion, Dymoke, entered Westminster Hall and threw down the gauntlet to challenge those who disputed the King's right to the crown. The suit worn on this occasion belonged originally to Sir Christopher Hatton, Captain of the Guard to Queen Elizabeth, and was made by Jacobe,[1] whose designs for armour have been referred to in Chapter III. The suit is now in the Guard Room at Windsor. The Guardia Nobile of the Pope still wear the picturesque half armour of the sixteenth century. The cuirass and helmet of the Household Cavalry of the present day are not survivals, for they were introduced at the time of the Coronation of George IV.

The study of defensive armour and weapons must of necessity need much careful comparison of examples and investigation of documentary evidence, but, even when undertaken only superficially, it will add greatly to the interest of modern history and of the arts of war. Costume can only be studied from pictorial and sculptured records, but in the case of armour we have, after a certain period, actual examples not only of historical but also of personal interest. With modern methods of arrangement and with the expert care of those most learned in this subject these examples will be an ever-present record which may be examined with more interest than might be bestowed upon many branches of the applied arts ; because, in addition to the interest centred in the personality of the wearers, we have the sure signs of the master-craftsman which are always evident in good craftsmanship, and, not infrequently, the sign-manual of the worker himself.

[1] Considered to be the same as Topf.

CHAPTER VII

WEAPONS

THE Sword. At the time of the Conquest the sword was straight, broad in blade, two-edged and pointed. The Quillons were straight and the grip ended in a Pommel which, as far as we

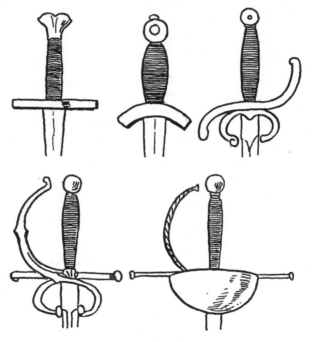

FIG. 46. Sword-hilts.

can judge from illustrated records, was square, round, lozenge-shaped or trefoiled (Fig. 46). There is not much change in the general lines of the sword during the twelfth century except in the form of the pommel.

In the thirteenth century the point, instead of starting abruptly at the extreme end of the blade, is of a more gradual form, showing that the use of the sword for thrusting was more general than in the previous centuries. The Grip seems to be very short for the proper balance of the weapon, if we may judge from those shown on Plate III, 1, 2, 3.

The quillons curve upwards towards the point and the pommel is frequently decorated with the badge or arms of the owner. The symbol of the Cross is frequently found on the sword-pommel. At this period the handle and scabbard are frequently enriched with

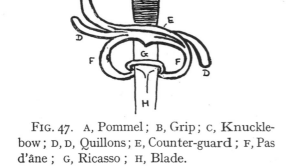

FIG. 47. A, Pommel; B, Grip; C, Knuckle-bow; D, D, Quillons; E, Counter-guard; F, Pas d'âne ; G, Ricasso ; H, Blade.

FIG. 48. Schiavona.

ornamental metal-work set with gems, as we find on the monument of King John in Worcester Cathedral. The cruciform shape of the sword-hilt continues through the fourteenth century without much radical change in its construction, but in the fifteenth century we find the 'Pas d'âne', which is formed of two rings curving above the quillons on each side of the Ricasso, or squared part of the blade above the hilt (Fig. 47). It is usual to describe the sword as it is held for use in the hand ; that is, with the point as the highest part and the pommel as the lowest. After the fifteenth century sword-play began to be studied as a science, and we find that, besides being used for offensive purposes, the sword-hilt was so designed as to be a defence in itself. From this we get all the guards and counterguards, which are so varied and intricate that it would require more space than is at our disposal to treat of them with any degree of completeness.

The type of sword that was thus developed by practice in its use was purely for thrusting purposes. The sword for cutting alone is generally simpler in form. The Cutilax, Falchion, Dussack, and Cutlas are all weapons of this order and generally have a simple hilt. The modern Claymore is really an adaptation of the Italian Schiavona (Fig. 48), and is in no way derived from the Claymore proper, the Two-hand sword of the Middle Ages. This great weapon, often as much as 6 feet in length from point to pommel, was used by foot-soldiers, and special military arrangements were made for the space given to its users, who required a good sweeping distance between each man (Fig. 49). The Hand-and-half sword is a variety of cross-hilted sword, in which the grip is sufficiently long for two or three fingers of the left hand to be used to assist the right hand in delivering a swinging cut.

FIG. 49.   Two-hand sword.

The early Dagger is of much the same form as the sword; it was worn on the right side with the sword on the left. One variety of the dagger was called the Miséricorde. It was finely pointed and, as its name grimly implies, was intended to penetrate the joints of the armour to give the *coup de grâce* to the fallen knight. The Main-gauche is also of the dagger order, but has a broad knuckle-guard and long straight quillons. It was used in conjunction with the rapier in duels with the point upwards, more as a means of warding off the sword-thrust than for actual stabbing. The Anelace and Cinquedea are broad-bladed short weapons used for stabbing only. The Baselard was the short sword carried by civilians in the fifteenth century.

Of staff weapons the principal is, of course, the Lance. At the time of the Conquest and up to the fourteenth century the shaft of the lance was of even thickness with lozenge- or leaf-shaped point. During the fourteenth century we find the shaft swelling just above the grip and then tapering below it. Plate XI, 14, shows the lance provided with a vamplate or shield, which protected the hand and made the right gauntlet unnecessary. Tilting lances are sometimes as much as 15 feet in length, and one specimen in the Tower weighs 20 lb. An engraving by Lucas Cranach (1472–1553), which depicts a tourney or mêlée of knights, shows the combatants preceded by squires on horseback who support these weighty lances till the moment of impact, when, it is presumed, they moved aside out of danger. The lance-point was sharp for active service, but for tournaments it was supposed to be blunted. This practice, however, was so often neglected that ordinances were framed enjoining the use of the Coronal or trefoiled button, which is shown on Plate XI, 15.

The other long-shafted staff weapons may be divided into those for stabbing and those for cutting. The Gisarme is a long-handled weapon which some writers consider to have been much the same as the Pole-axe. From Wace we learn that it was sharp, long, and broad.[1] It was in all probability a primitive form of the Bill. This was also a broad-bladed weapon and was used only by foot-soldiers. It seems to have been evolved from the agricultural scythe. The Godendag was the name given by the Flemings to the Halbard. It had an axe-blade with curved or straight spikes at the back and a long point to terminate the shaft. In this detail it differed from the pole-axe. The halbard proper was used as early as the thirteenth century and appears in the designs from the Painted Chamber at Westminster figured

[1] '. . . granz gisarmes esmolues' (*Roman de Rou*, l. 12907).
'. . . gisarmes lunges è lées' (ib., l. 13431).

by Stothard.[1] From the seventeenth century onwards it was used only for ceremonial purposes and was richly decorated. It was carried on parade by infantry drum-majors in England as late as 1875. It was much favoured by the Swiss, who armed the front rank of the footmen with this weapon. Those used for parade purposes are elaborately engraved on the blades, while the shafts are often covered with velvet and studded with gilded nails. These ornate weapons are used still by the Gentlemen-at-Arms on State occasions. The Voulge is a primitive weapon evolved from an agricultural implement of the same class as the hedging bill in use at the present day. The Lochaber axe is of much the same form ; its distinguishing feature being the hook at the top of the shaft, which was used in scaling walls. The Glaive is also a broad-bladed weapon, but where the bill and gisarme are more or less straight towards the edge, the glaive curves backwards. It is often to be found richly engraved for show purposes. In French writings the word glaive is sometimes loosely used for lance or sword.

The stabbing or thrusting long-shafted weapons include the Lance, Spear, and Javelin. After these the most important is the Pike. This is very similar to the spear, but was used exclusively by foot-soldiers. In the seventeenth century it was carried by infantry interspersed among the arquebusiers. There are several works on pike-drill and treatises on its management. Lord Orrery, in his *Art of War*, comments on the differences in length and recommends that all should be 16½ feet long. The shaft was made of seasoned ash and the head was fastened with two cheeks of iron, often 4 feet long, which ran down the shaft to prevent the head being cut off by cavalry. At the butt-end was a spike for sticking into the ground when resisting cavalry. In a treatise entitled *The Art of Training* (1662) directions are given that the 'grip' of the shaft should be covered with velvet to afford a sure hold for the hand. This grip was called the Armin. There are also suggestions that a tassel should be fixed midway to prevent the rain running down the shaft and so causing the hand to slip. When we consider that

---

[1] *Monumenta Vetusta*, vol. vi.

PLATE XI

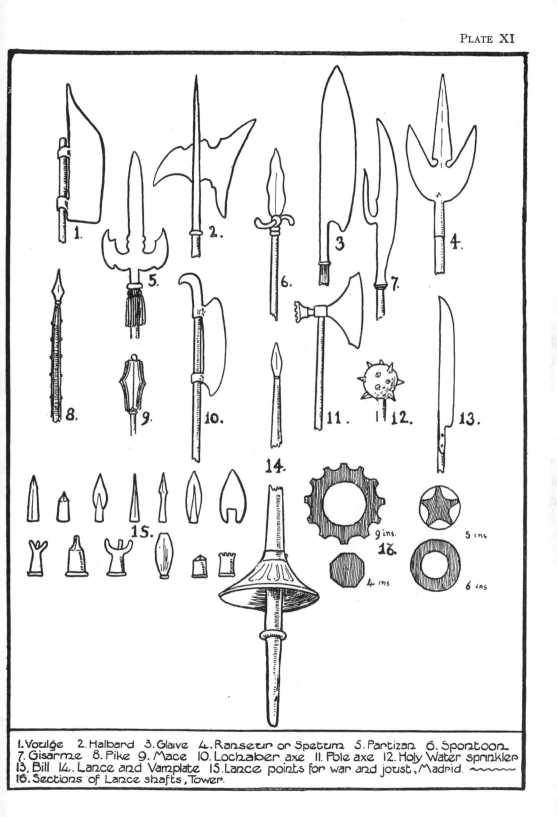

1. Voulge 2. Halbard 3. Glaive 4. Ranseur or Spetum 5. Partizan 6. Spontoon
7. Gisarme 8. Pike 9. Mace 10. Lochaber axe 11. Pole axe 12. Holy Water sprinkler
13. Bill 14. Lance and Vamplate 15. Lance points for war and joust, Madrid.
16. Sections of Lance shafts, Tower.

the pikeman had to keep the cavalry at bay while the arquebusier was reloading—a lengthy process—we can understand the importance of these regulations. The pike was carried by the colour-sergeants in the British Army at the beginning of the nineteenth century, and was last used in the French Army in 1789. The Spontoon is a species of half-pike, which was carried by the colour-sergeants in the British Army up to the end of the eighteenth century, if not longer. The Spetum and the Ranseur are often confused. The names are usually given to those weapons which

have sharp lateral projections fixed at a more or less acute angle to the point. They could not be used for cutting, but used for thrusting they inflicted terrible wounds. The Partizan is somewhat of the same order, but is known best in museums in its decorated form as used in ceremonial parades. These show-weapons were used by the Judge's guard in Oxford up to 1875, and are still carried by the Yeomen of the Guard on State occasions.

FIG. 50. Morning Star.

The Bayonet, although introduced in France in 1647, is so essentially a part of the firearm that we need do no more than mention it among the thrusting weapons. The scope of this work will not allow of any notice of firearms ; that subject, owing to modern developments, is too wide to be treated in a few sentences.

Of short-handled weapons the Club or Mace is to be found on the Bayeux Tapestry, and is generally quatrefoil or heart-shaped at the head. The mace was the weapon of militant ecclesiastics, who thus escaped the denunciation against 'those who fight with the sword'. It is generally supposed that the Gibet was of the same order. Wace, in the *Roman de Rou* (line 13459), writes :—

> Et il le gibet seisi
> Ki a sun destre bras pendi.

The mace was usually carried slung by a loop to the saddle-bow or on the right wrist, so that, when sword or lance were lost, it could be used at once. A less ornamental weapon is the Holy-water Sprinkler. This is formed of a ball of iron studded with sharp projecting spikes, and fixed upon a long or short handle. The Morning Star is akin to the Military Flail, a weapon derived from the agricultural implement of that name. It is much the same as the Holy-water Sprinkler, except that the spiked ball is not socketed on the handle but hangs from a chain (Fig. 50). The names of these two weapons are often transposed, but we propose to adhere to the nomenclature used in the Tower Armouries as being more likely to be correct. The War-hammer and Battle-axe need but little description. They were generally used by horsemen, and their general form only varies in detail from implements in use at the present day. The Pole-axe was a weapon in great request for jousting on foot, in the 'champ clos'. The blade is much like the halbard, but at the back is a hammer-shaped projection with a roughened surface.

The Longbow may be said to have gained the battles of Senlac, Crecy, and Agincourt, and so ranks as one of the most important of English weapons. It was from $5\frac{1}{2}$ to 6 feet in length and was made of yew, or, when this wood was scarce, of witch hazel. It is a popular tradition in the country that the yew-trees which were so important for the manufacture of this weapon were grown in churchyards because they were poisonous to cattle, and the church-yards were the only fenced-in spaces. There is, however, no documentary evidence to support this. The string was of hemp or silk. The archer carried twenty-four ' clothyard ' shafts in his belt and wore a wrist-guard called a Bracer to protect his wrist from the recoil of the string. These bracers were of ivory or leather and were often decorated. The arrows were tipped with the goose-quill, but Roger Ascham, in his *Toxophilus*, writes that peacock arrows were used ' for gayness '. So notable were the English bow-makers for their productions that in 1363 we find the Pope sending to this country for bows.

The Crossbow or Arbalest is first heard of in the twelfth century,

and at this date was considered so 'unfair' a weapon that the
Popes forbade its use.   Innocent II in 1139 fulminated against this
barbarous weapon, but allowed of its use by Christians against
Infidels.   By the end of the thirteenth century, however, it was in
general use.   At first the crossbow was strung by hand; but when
it was made more powerful, mechanical means had to be resorted
to to bend the bow, which was often of steel.   There are two
varieties of war crossbows : that strung with the 'goat's-foot' lever,

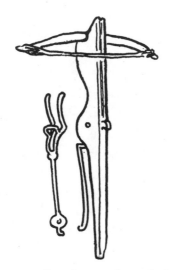

FIG. 51.   Crossbow and goat's-foot lever.   FIG. 52.   Crossbow and windlass.

which is shown on Fig. 51, and a heavier kind called the arbalest
'*à tour*', which was strung with a cog-wheel and ratchet arrangement called the Moulinet or windlass (Fig. 52).   The arbalest
'*à cric*' is a larger form of this variety.   The archer using these
heavy weapons was entrenched behind a Pavis or shield fixed
in the ground as shown on Fig. 37.   The Quarel or bolt used
for the crossbow is shorter and thicker than that used for the
longbow.

Of the other projectile-hurling weapons, such as the Fustibal or
Sling, the different forms of Catapult used in siege operations, and
the innumerable varieties of firearm, we have no space to write.
The former, being mostly fashioned of wood and cordage, are seldom

to be met with in museums, and we can only judge of their design and use from illuminated miniatures and paintings. The firearm, being, as it is, subject to further development, cannot be taken into full consideration in this work except so far as it affected the defensive armour and in time ousted the staff-weapon.

With this bare enumeration of the principal weapons in use from the twelfth to the eighteenth century we draw our all too meagre notes to a conclusion. The subject is so vast, because each example is distinct in itself and because no general rule holds absolutely good for all, that many volumes might be produced with advantage on each epoch of the defences and weapons of Europe. No better advice to the would-be student can be given than that of Baron de Cosson in the Introduction to the Catalogue of Helmets and Mail (*Arch. Journ.*, vol. xxxvii). He writes : ' For the study of ancient armour to be successfully pursued it is of primary importance that a careful examination be made of every existing specimen within our reach. . . . Every rivet-hole and rivet in a piece must be studied and its use and object thought out. The reasons for the varied forms, thicknesses, and structure of the different parts must have special attention. . . . This alone will enable us to derive full profit from our researches into ancient authors and our examination of ancient monuments. This pre-liminary study will alone enable us to form a sound opinion on two important points. First, the authority to be accorded to any given representation of armour in ancient art . . . whether it was copied from real armour or whether it was the outcome of the artist's imagination ; and also whether a piece of existing armour is genuine or false, and whether or no it is in its primitive condition.'

To this may be added that in studying armour at its best epoch, that is during the fifteenth century, we find the dignity of true craftsmanship proclaimed, and utility and grace attained without the addition of that so-called decoration which with the advent of the Renaissance was the bane of all the crafts.

INDEX